RESISTANCE MOVEMENTS IN NORTH-EAST INDIA

The Jaintias of Meghalaya 1860-1863

Dr. Shobhan N. Lamare

2022

Regency Publications

A Division of

Astral International Pvt. Ltd.

New Delhi - 110 002

First Published, 2001
Reprinted, 2022

ISBN: 978-81-87498-42-1 (Hardbound)

Published by : **Regency Publications**
A Division of
Astral International Pvt. Ltd.
– ISO 9001:2008 Certified Company –
4760-61/23, Ansari Road
Darya Ganj, New Delhi - 110 002
Phone: 011-4354 9197, 2327 8134
Fax: +91-11-2324 3060
E-mail: info@astralint.com
Website: www.astralint.com

Digitally Printed at : **Replika Press Pvt. Ltd.**

For Émi

To reflect back sometimes
on what had happened

Foreword

In early 1860, the Jaintias, concerned that the British Indian government had imposed a house tax on them, the collection of which had started some months earlier, and further aggravated by the restrictions on their local customs, rose in resistance to the imperial power. What started as a localized upheaval soon spread over the entire Jaintia Hills. Suppressed in a few months the Khasi and Jaintia Hills district and Bengal provincial authorities were caught unaware when the Jaintias rose in resistance again in January 1862. In suppressing the first phase of the resistance, the British officials acts of restricting the traditional ways of the people and then imposing an income tax on this largely pastoral and agricultural community, drove them into an even more fierce and long drawn armed movement which involved the entire populace and threatened to spread beyond the hills. It would be another two years and more before the "little war" as it was called, was finally suppressed, not by negotiation but by the imperial power's military might.

The author has taken a significant aspect of the history of the tribe and given its detail. He has gone beyond the earlier studies of what was largely military history to see the people's perspective. This he has done by judicious use of Jaintia oral history, weaving these sources with archival and published references. He traces the origins of the upheaval to the annexation of the hills into the East India Company dominion in 1835, the informal nature of Company rule between its annexation and 1860 when the first phase of the resistance occurred. The possible influence of the deposed Jaintia Raja, the impact of the Indian revolt of 1857 are some of the other interesting connections that have been researched in this history. The British military operations and the nature of Jaintia war tactics is presented in great detail but not without loosing focus on the central issue of presenting a tribal resistance to alien rule.

Doctoral dissertations are the result of much planning, hard and sustained research and does not come without financial inputs. It would be a shame given the enormous effort put into their presentation should they end up as just another dissertation on a university library shelf. The author, Shobhan N. Lamare has taken pains to research on a viable problem in regional history, then go through the thesis he submitted for examination and prepare it for publication. This has been an attempt to integrate the history of a small tribe into the history of modern India. It will encourage him and countless others in India's North-East to have their histories incorporated into and referred in the general and thematic histories of India. With the publication of yet another of our scholar's research, the Department of History, North-Eastern Hill University, takes pride in the training and encouragement it has given over the years to young historians and their contribution to our understanding of the past.

10 April 2001

Dr. David Reid Syiemlieh
Professor of History
NEHU, Shillong

Preface

Though articles on the Jaintias and their resistance had appeared in journals and edited texts, yet there is no single monograph on the resistance movement which the people had carried out in their fight against the British between 1860–1863. The studies that had so far been carried out, no doubt gave direction to the problem, but since they had compounded their studies into just few pages, they have not thrown sufficient light on the contribution of the people for a national cause. This study, therefore, seeks to understand the problem from a wider and more detailed perspective. The different armed resistance movements that had taken place in the region against the English East India Company and the British have been highlighted chronologically as a prelude to this study, as also to place the Jaintia resistance within the context of British Imperialism.

This history fits into the broader studies and trends that have been done in recent years to study and understand the various forms of resistance movements against the English East India Company and the Raj. This new trend in historical enquiry has given a new dimension to the interaction between the British administrator and their Indian subjects. In part the new direction comes as an expression of the post colonial histories and the opening up of archives to materials, hitherto closed for research. The colonial-Indian interaction has come under critical scrutiny in an attempt to show that all the British did was not in the interest of their subjects. In the light of this background, the study of the resistance, becomes all the more significant in today's approach to the study of the past.

Here it may be pointed out that the term 'resistance' will be preferred to 'rebellion'. Rebellion indicates that a level of authority is imposed on people before their reaction. In the case of the Jaintias, though their kingdom was annexed in 1835, the influence of the British authority over this community was negligible and therefore, when the first real efforts were made by the British to impose their rule, the Jaintias resisted. The work is an attempt to look into the details of the resistance and especially into the courses and the aftermath which has been largely ignored, and in this regard attention was also given to the role of U Kiang Nangbah in providing leadership in the second phase of the resistance.

The present work is the outcome of my doctoral thesis submitted to the North-Eastern Hill University in 1999 under the title "The Jaintia Resistance of 1860–1863". During the course of my research work I had consulted at length the archival materials and though reliable, the same were scrutinised and cross examined with the use of Jaintia oral traditions. Field study and interviews were also conducted.

I take this opportunity to convey my sincere thanks and gratitude to my supervisor Dr. David Reid Syiemlieh for his valuable guidance at all levels of the research. I also thank him for the time and the interest he has taken through my research work. I am also grateful to him for the foreword of this book.

I also wish to thank and acknowledge the libraries and archivists at the Jawaharlal Nehru Museum and Library, Teen Murthi, New Delhi; the National Archives of India, Janpath, New Delhi; the West Bengal State Archives, Guwahati and the North-Eastern Hill University Library.

I also wish to thank Dr. C.J. Thomas, Deputy Director, ICSSR-NERC for the interest he took in the publishing of this book. Finally, my thanks go to Mr. A.K. Varma of Regency Publication for undertaking the publication of this work.

A special thank also goes to the Principal of St. Edmund's College, Rev. Bro. E.V. Miranda for encouraging me to complete the research by granting me leave to collect the historical data. I am also very grateful to my colleague Mr. Osmond Kharmawphlang for drawing a sketch map of the period under study. It also goes to my friends both far and near who were instrumental in providing information about the oral traditions, for without their help the work would have been incomplete.

To my parents and family members I owe a great deal for all the support and help which they have rendered in more than one occasion. Words are inadequate to express my deep sense of gratitude towards them.

I am deeply grateful to my wife Jennifer who helped me in reading the draft and worked many long nights typing it. Also for bearing with me when I have sacrificed my attention at home on holidays while I wrote and travelled.

I trust the book will stimulate interest in the mind of the readers and provoke further research works on the Jaintias and other people of the region.

Shillong
5, April 2001

Shobhan N. Lamare

Contents

Glossary

Batta	—	Discount
Burkandaze	—	Armed retainer
Chokey	—	Outpost
Chnong	—	Village
Chad Pastieh	—	Annual Jaintia sword and shield dance festival
Chowkidars	—	Gate keepers
Dikus	—	Outsiders
Diwani	—	Right to collect revenue
Dalois	—	The traditional chiefs in the Jaintia Hills
Dkhar	—	Foreigner
Durbar	—	An assembly
Daroga	—	A police constable
Elaka	—	An administrative or territorial Jurisdiction
Ghat	—	River port
Hindustani	—	Indian
Hat	—	Market
Hima	—	Kingdom
Havildar	—	A non-commissioned army officer
Hondia	—	Spirit
Jamedar	—	Custodian
Kurs	—	Clans
Kunwar	—	Heirs of the ex-Raja
Kattra-taka	—	Jaintia coins

Lathiyal	—	Armed retainers
Lathis	—	Sticks
Langdoh	—	Priests
Musnud	—	To place in power
Mantri	—	Minister
Maulvi	—	Muslim priests
Maund	—	Weight
Moonsiff	—	Revenue official
Mohur	—	Gold coin
Mukteer	—	An official or a spokesman
Naick	—	Rank of junior army officer
Panchayat	—	Village tribunal
Panji	—	Bamboo spike
Poligar	—	Landed military magnates in south India
Pandit	—	Hindu priests
Pator	—	Deputy of the Daloi
Ryot	—	People
Raid	—	Provinces
Raja	—	King
Sardar	—	Head of an administrative unit
Sudder Ameen	—	Court
Syiem	—	Chief; in the case of the Jaintias it is equivalent to king
Subehdar	—	Rank of junior army officer
Sunnad	—	A written authority
Sangot	—	An administrtative officer in the Jaintia Hills
Sepoy	—	Soldier
Thakur	—	God
Tup	—	Cannon
Tehsildar	—	A revenue officer
Thana	—	Jail
Vakil	—	Lawyer
Wasan	—	Elder
Zamindar	—	Landlord

A SKETCH MAP OF JAINTIA HILLS
1860 - 1863

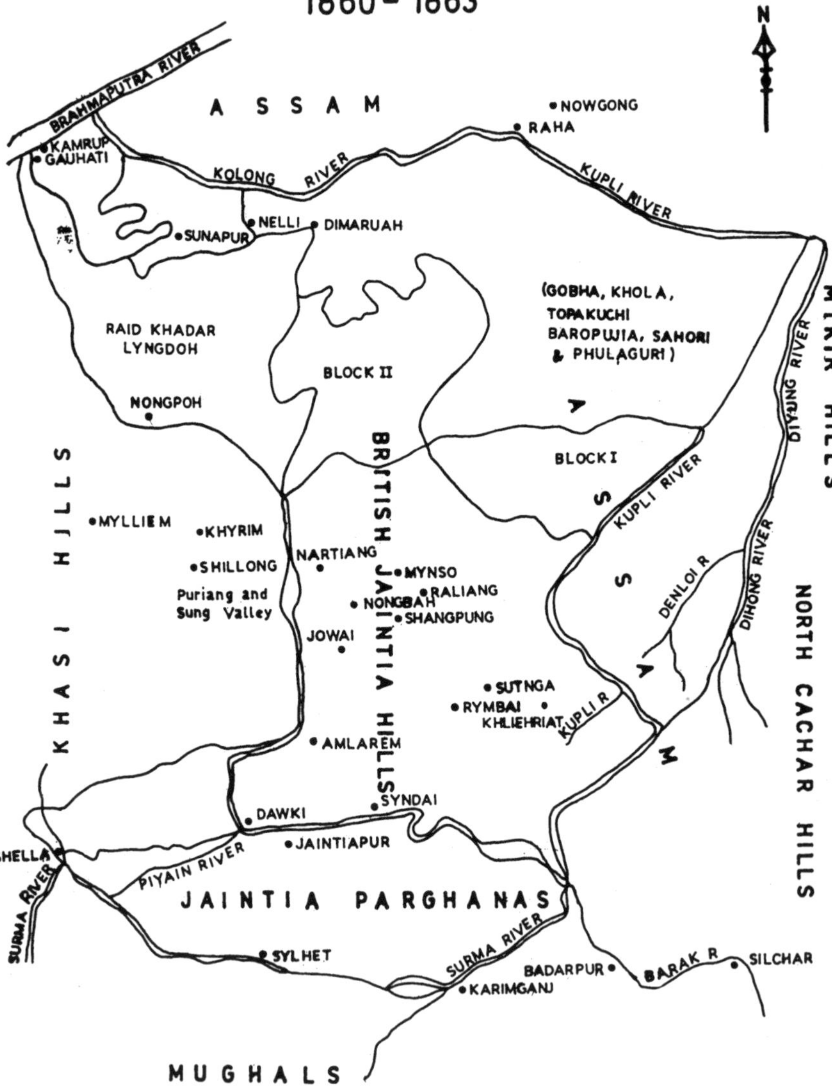

1

Resistance Movements in British India—An Overview

In recent years historians have turned their attention to a study of various forms of resistance movements and rebellions against the English East India Company and the British Raj. This trend in historical enquiry has given a new dimension to the interaction between the British administration and their Indian subjects. In part, the new direction comes as an expression of the post-colonial histories and the opening up of archives to materials hitherto closed for research. Secondly, the colonial Indian interaction has come under critical scrutiny in an attempt to show that not all that the British did was in the interest of their subjects. A study of resistance or rebellion movements, therefore, becomes significant in today's approach of the study of the past.

Self assertion has been an important phenomena in modern India. Such developments have brought about new elements of thoughts particularly in understanding the political nature of the period under study. The lack of contentment of the peasants as well as of the tribal populace had given rise to aggressive actions. Their resistance movements were motivated by the peoples' discontent against a variety of impositions by the British in their way of life. Some movements went beyond mere resistance to administrative measures to press for the end of the British rule over their specific geographical areas. The study under review, *i.e.*, the Jaintia in resistance will show, as the work develops that what started as a reaction to administrative and other measures became an attempt by the Jaintia to assert their freedom.

The clash of interest between people and an authority is rather a complex and a sensitive issue. The problem should not be seen from the British perspective alone, where in most cases the tribal unrest to take a case, was taken up from the policemen's approach.[1] The tribal movements on the fact of it may appear to be political movements in their tone and temper and would seem that the immediate objective of such movements was to gain political control. Armed movements if analysed properly may reveal the grievances which the people have been suppressing for years. Therefore, in this context it would not be fair if the British perspective alone would be allowed to generalise for the whole structure of a movement.[2] In the case of the Jaintias, integrated study have been carried out and it is particularly for this reason that a case study on the people becomes all the more important.

To have a clear picture of the problem in study, it is necessary to look into the other movements that reacted to British rule. The events of the 15th and 16th centuries accompanied by geographical discoveries had resulted in the discovery of new lands, countries and continents by many European adventurers. The frequent contacts between these people led to the growth of trade and commerce and also the acquisition of lands. India in this manner was also thrown open to trade and commerce with the countries of the west. There was tremendous rivalry amongst the different European powers to obtain trade concessions from the central and provincial rulers. In this struggle among the different western trading companies, the English East India Company was successful in defeating the other trading rivals, the Dutch, the Portuguese and the French. By 1818 almost the whole of India was under the control of the English East India Company and the Mughals had receded in their importance into the background together with regional powers who had benefitted briefly from the political collapse of the Mughals.

The change in power and authority brought about radical changes in the Indian sub-continent. The British though they were rulers, did not identify themselves with the Indians and had largely remained alien to this land. This led to a sharp contrast between the rulers and the ruled or between the exploiters and the exploited. By the 1850s changes started to appear in many facets of life. There were changes in the administration and the new courts and legal system added confusion in the minds of the people. The prevalence of corruption in the police and judicial departments created more problems to the existing ones. Changes in administration, on the other hand, led to the ruin of the traditional rulers and also to those who depended on them for financial assistance. The case of the artisans, scholars, pandits, *maulvis* and other men of art and literature may be included as being affected by the new rule. The process of commercialization did not even spare the tribal economy. The tribal areas were swamped by the outsiders from the plains like the money lenders, traders, land grabbers, contractors and others. Adding to this the British legal conceptions of absolute private property disturbed the traditional joint ownership and sharpened tensions within the tribal society.[3]

The tribal societies were also greatly disturbed in their abstract concepts, when the missionaries who accompanied the rulers started to contradict the very notions on which their society was based. These drastic changes in the attitudes and ideas of the people resulted in uneasiness and often ended in open hostilities. It was in part because of these developments and resentment to change that the revolt of 1857 had broken out. It was considered to be "traditional India's struggle against foreign rule".[4] Though the process of colonization and consolidation was carried out by the British, it had never been an easy task for them. The element of resentment was very much there with the people and at times it had led to serious armed resistance movements. There were numerous instances when these resistances would be carried out only by the deposed *Rajas* and *Nawabs* or their descendants, or sometimes by the uprooted and impoverished *zamindars*, landlords, the *poligars* (landed military magnates in South India) and ex-retainers and officials of the conquered Indian States.[5] These people in most cases were supported by the peasants, ruined artisans and demobilized soldiers.

The extraction of land revenue in a manner where the motive was to collect "as large an amount as possible produced a veritable upheaval in Indian villages".[6] After the battle of Plassey (1757) the British had established their authority in Bengal and it was from here that the first reaction against them could be seen. It may be recalled that in 1763 the Sanyasi Rebellion broke out in Bengal, and was mainly carried out by the displaced peasants and demobilized soldiers and was led by religious monks. This movement was made famous by Bankim Chandra Chatterjee in his novel *Anand Math*.[7] After this another opposition came but from a different quarter altogether. The opposition came from Mir Qasim the successor of Mir Jafar where he pointed out to the Calcutta Council about the activities of the English merchants at the expense of the Indians and at the same time avoiding the internal tariff which was due to his government. The members of the Council did not pay any close attention to his objections. The *Nawab,* therefore, abolished all internal tariff so that his subjects might not suffer. This ultimately led to a war between the British and the combined forces of Mir Qasim, Shah Alam and Suja-ud-Daulah. The English equipped with better weapons defeated the combined forces in the battle of Bauxar, 1764. This did not end the opposition, in fact it was the beginning of a series of resistance movements which broke out in different parts of the country and carried on till the early part of the 20th century.

The grievances of the people of the Chittagong Hill Tracts was expressed when they started an armed resistance movement in 1776 by rejecting British rule. This came about mainly when the tribals found out that their way of life was adversely affected by the Government officials. Interference in their traditional landholding system and the enhancing of revenues was greatly resented. The region *i.e.,* the entire Chittagong Hill Tract was inhabited by the Kukis, Khyongs, Pankos which anthropologically falls under one ethnic group called the Kukis. Another major tribe was the Tipperahs. Ever since the Chittagong province was brought under the control of the Mughals from 1666[8] onwards, the Mugs and the Chakmas, the two leading Arakanese tribes were added to the list. The Mugs were the arch rivals of the Mughals, whereas the Chakmas showed friendly disposition. Due to this type of differences the Chakmas were resented by the Mugs. They left lower Chittagong and settled in the Hill Tracts under the protection of the Mughal Government. The Mughal officers collected revenues from the Chakmas and the Kukis in kind; since the area was not under the influence of money economy. Usually cotton amounting to 500 maunds were collected annually. The Mughals treated the province as a military outpost against the Arakanese Mugs rather than as a source of revenue.The rent-free land which the people were enjoying underwent a change when the area came under the control of the English East India Company. New land measure system were introduced in order to increase the revenue of the Company. These measures provoked the hill chiefs and the people and an armed resistance broke out in 1776. The Chakmas and the Kukis fought hand in hand against the British. Between 1777 to 1781, three full scale military expeditions were sent against the tribals under the command of European officers[9] but all attempts to suppress them failed. The problem was solved when the British were successful in bringing a rift between the two groups by treating the Kukis to be ethnically different from the Chakmas. The Kukis were easily impressed and the rift between the two turned into a chasm. By February 1787, a peace treaty was signed and the British recognised the Kuki chief Juan Baksh as the *Zamindar*.[10]

Another formidable uprising made its appearance in Rangpur in Bengal in 1783, when the peasants started to demonstrate against the new farming experiments launched by the Company's Government.[11] The peasants, both Hindus and Muslims fought side by side against the Company's official. This assumed the character of an armed peasant rebellion.[12]

In 1830, the British control over Orissa was extended but this was not to go without opposition. The very next year *i.e.*, in 1804, the *Raja* of Khurda revolted against the British but was suppressed with a heavy hand by the Government. It remained quiet for sometime, but very soon the *Paiks* of Khurda started to show their resentment once again. The revenue collectors and police were attacked and the government treasury was set ablaze. It was after resorting to repressive measures, that the government finally managed to bring control over Khurda in 1817. It was only in 1825 that the revolt in Khurda was finally suppressed and the *Raja* of Khurda was given a pension and allowed to live in Cuttack.[13]

Hostilities also broke out in Madras in the Khond Mahal where the Khonds lived. It started in 1815 in a place named Gumsar between the British and the local ruler Dhanajay Bhari. The *Raja* was arrested and his state was occupied by the British. Bhari appealed to the Khonds for help and the Khonds under the leadership of Dora Bisui revolted. The revolt was however suppressed but not for long. Much later in 1864 the Khonds revolted again under the new leadership of Chakra Bisui but this resistance was not successful. The Khonds were defeated and their territory was transferred from Madras to Orissa for political administration.[14]

After the Anglo-Burmese War of 1824–26, the British came into closer contact with a number of hill tribes in the north east region.[15] Though at first it took the form of an understanding with the British against the forces of Ava, but later because of the repeated incursions, differences came about which finally led to armed conflicts. In this regard the case of the Khasi resistance of 1829 under the leadership of U Tirot Sing may be referred to. The hostilities between the Khasis and the British came about mainly on the following issues. The complaints of eight Khasi states to David Scott, the then Political Agent about the transfer to the Company of lowlands on the northern foothills did not receive much attention. Though it was claimed by the Khasi chiefs that these lands were part of the Khasi states in the hill, the British officials following the conquest of Assam and the expulsion of the Burmese started to collect revenue from these tracts. No decision was arrived at which the rights of the Khasis was considered.[16] It was also seen that David Scott had exploited the situation in order to get the *Syiem* of Nongkhlaw to allow the road to pass through his state. "The growing British interest in the hills, their treaty relations with those states which agreed to the road, the growing establishments at Nongkhlaw and Cherrapunji, their control of Sylhet and Assam must have created a psychosis of fear among the Khasis which burst into the massacre at Nongkhlaw."[17] It was only with the surrender of U Tirot Sing on 13 January 1833,[18] on the condition that his life be spared[19] that the Khasi resistance came to an end. Tirot

Sing was taken to Gauhati and eventually confined to house arrest in Dacca where he passed away on 17 July 1835.[20]

Between 1831–32 there was trouble in the Chota Nagpur plateau. The tribesmen better known as the Kols were up in arms against the non-tribal adventures who had been exploiting them for sometime. The insurrection began in the Sonepur Pargana bordering Singhbhum and was joined by the Larka Kols of Kolhan.[21] At first it was not that serious but seeing that there was no resistance from the non-tribals and the British troops were not readily available to check the uprising the Kols became more violent and soon there was an orgy of slaughter and arson which drove the non-tribal out of the Kol land. This subsequently brought the Kols into conflict with the authorities. In the process the *chowkidars* and the *darogas* were attacked and killed. The *thanas* were burnt. Revenue collectors were not spared. Troops had to come from Barrackpur and Danapur. The Kols resorted to guerrilla warfare. At times the Kols would inflict seven cuts on some of their victims on account of the seven new taxes imposed on them. One for *batta* (discount) on changing copper for silver, the second for the excise tax on spirits (*handia*), the third for the proposed tax on opium, the fourth for the fines for supposed or real crimes, the fifth for village *salami,* the sixth for the forced labour on the roads and the seventh for the postal taxes on the village.[22] The houses of the money lenders, grain merchants, farmers of land, salt dealers and other non-tribals were special targets of attack. Thousands of them were massacred before British authority could be re-imposed.[23]

The Akas, the Daphlas and the Miris tribes residing beyond Tezpur and North Lakhimpur[24] borders of Assam, also created problems for the British. There were problems in the Aka region in 1830 and in the Daphlas and Miris habited hills between 1838–1839. The Abors (Adis) on the other hand inhibit the outer ranges of the eastern Himalayas. It was in 1848 that trouble started. It originated over the gold washing pursuits of the Miris and Cacharis who worked in the rivers flowing out of the hills. The Abors asserted their right to a percentage of gold and fish taken from rivers flowing from their hills. Since this was not complied, a raid into the Miris and Cacharis settlements was carried out. The 2nd Assam

Light Infantry from Sadiya followed up the raiders and burnt their villages. A series of retaliatory raids and outrages were carried out with intervals for many years upto 1911.[25]

North Cachar witnessed a revolt between 1841–1844 when Tularam Senapati decided to challenge the British authorities when his district was taken over by the East India Company. The revolt was carried out with a motive of gaining back the territory which he had lost. For one and half years the detachment of the Cachar levy was employed to suppress the uprising. It was only in 1844 when Tularam surrendered that the fight came to an end. As a consequence of this, the district was placed under Asaloo, 15 miles east of Haflong for all acts of administration.[26] A small civil staff along with a strong detachment of the levy was posted in the region.

Encounters between the Nagas and the Company authorities had been frequent. The strongest among the Angami Naga villages were those of Mezoma; Khonoma, Jatsoma and others. Aggression into the plains were frequent and in 1849 the authorities felt the necessity of having an outpost at Mezoma to check these raids. At first the headmen of Mezoma and Khonoma agreed with the *daroga* Bogchand on the location of the outpost and even told the people to start building the stockade for it. Trouble started when Bogchand started to enquire about men who were involved in recent raids. These people being identified, he immediately arrested them. On his return to Samaguting, while on a night halt at Piphima Boghcnad's party was attacked from all sides. Twenty-two *sepoys* were killed at Piphima and those who managed to escape were slayed in their pursuit. On hearing the news a military expedition under Captain Vincent with 150 men of the 2nd Assam Light Infantry moved into the hills. The force entered the Naga hills on the early part of the winter of 1849–1850. Captain Vincent's contingent was attacked and at one camp, lost a large amount of stores. He however had to return because of ill health. It was only on March 1850 that Vincent and Butler along with Lt. Campbell accompanied by a stronger detachment of the Assam Light Infantry, the Cachar Levy and the Jorhat Militia, re-entered the hills and attacked both Mezoma and Khonoma[27] and defeated them. Matter did not end here. In fact, the Nagas continued with their sporadic raids till the early part of the 20th century.[28]

The Santhal uprising was another important incident amongst the numerous other tribal revolts. They revolted in 1855. The Santhals belonged to Manbhum, Barabhum, Hazaribagh, Birbhum, Midnapur and Bankura areas. They left their ancestral home on account of the oppressive demands made by the *zamindars* after the Permanent Settlement of Bengal in 1793.[29] They migrated to the hilly tracts of Rajmahal hills.[30] Their poverty and simplicity was taken advantage of by the revenue collectors, money lenders, *zamindars,* the court officials and the police. Instead of helping the peasants, the Government seemed to be party in this oppression. It was because of all these that the Santhals "made a determined attempt to expel the outsiders—the *dikus*—and proclaimed the complete annihilation of the alien regime."[31] The Santhals considered the *dikus* and government servants to be morally corrupt and given to begging, stealing, lying and drunkenness.[32] They became convinced that unless they could wrest their lands from the government there would be no end to their sufferings.

By 1854, stray cases of attacking and robbing the *zamindars* and money lenders began to occur. On July 1855, they marched to Calcutta to place their petition before the government to free them from their oppressors, but their movements were obstructed by a Government Inspector. This led to violence and their resultant massacre at the hands of the British. Soon nearly 60,000 Santhals had been mobilized and were led by Sido and Kanhu who claimed that *Thakur* (god) had communicated with them and told them to take up arms and to fight for their independence.[33] The Government on realising the scale of the rebellion organised a major military campaign against the Santhals. It mobilised a military force under the command of a Major General, declared martial law in the affected areas and offered rewards upto Rs. 10,000 for the capture of various leaders. The rebellion was crushed ruthlessly and more than 15,000 lost their lives and their villages destroyed. Sido was betrayed and was captured and killed in August 1855, while Kanhu was arrested in February 1866.[34]

As a result of the rebellion the Santhal area which had been previously administratively broken up and merged into the neighbouring districts, was recognized into a separate entity known as the Santhal Parganas and a special type of administration was introduced there. The uprising therefore was partially successful. The 'Santhal Revolt' had its repercussions in other parts of the country. The Indigo strike of 1860, the Pabna and Bogra uprising of 1872, and the Maratha peasant uprising in Poona and Ahmednagar in 1875–76 may be mentioned.

Interestingly, before May 1857,[35] which signalled the outbreak of the uprising of 1857, the Bheels, a section of the war-like community of central India, scattered mostly in the western Ghats, took up arms against the British government. They were stirred by the news of the rebellion against the East India Company's Government. Their main stronghold was Kandesh. The Bheels under the leadership of Kajee Singh, Bhagoji Naik and others raised the standard of revolt and directed their attacks against the British Government in Kandesh. It was a mass rising where more than 2000 Bheels under the leadership of six Naiks united in the neighbourhood of Kandesh alone.[36] This revolt was put to an end in the early part of 1858.

The years following the great uprising of 1857–58 was marked by financial strains on the part of the British Government in India. It was estimated that the cost of the suppression of the rebellion amounted to 40 million pounds.[37] Therefore, the policies of the British government in India went for radical change and restructured the taxation policy including the land revenue. This was carried out mainly with the intention to realise the expenses which had been incurred in suppressing the uprising. P.N. Banerjee has pointed out that the deficit in the budget of 1858–1859 "exceeded fourteen million pounds sterlings".[38] Therefore, "to restore order in public accounts" and "to balance the income and expenditure"[39] was the task which the government addressed immediately after the suppression. In order to meet their imperial interest, James Wilson, a political economist, who was Financial Secretary to the Treasury of England was sent to India to restructure the Indian finance. He brought three major changes:

(a) he introduced a state paper currency; (b) a licence tax, and (c) the income tax. All these were introduced in 1860.[40] These arrangements led to serious resentments among various sections of the Indian people and aggravated the tensions that were already seething. Therefore, the events after 1857–1858 and the uprising that followed have to be seen from this perspective.

The events of 1857 had hardly settled when the indigo cultivators of Bengal revolted between 1850 and 1861. In this revolt the initiative came from the peasants themselves. The main centre of this uprising came from the district of Nadi, but it spread to the other districts of Jessore, Khulna, Murshidabad and Malda. In Bengal the cultivation of indigo was introduced by the European planters in the last quarter of the 18th century. It was for the first time that English capital was invested in this industry.[41] The annual crop was cultivated for its dye and the English indigo merchants used to earn fabulous profits by exporting indigo to Europe.[42] One pound of indigo in the English market was sold between Rs. 5–7 and the same was purchased from the peasants at Re. 1 and annas 4 only.[43] Lured by this profits in indigo cultivation the English East India Company began to take direct part in indigo cultivation from 1780 onwards. Indigo manufactures were brought from West Indies and began to extend the cultivation of indigo. Gradually a class of European indigo planters grew in Bengal, Bihar and other parts of India. Indian cultivators were employed for this extensive cultivation. The plantation of indigo was fabulous for the Europeans but for the cultivators it was an unashamed form of their exploitation and violent oppression.[44]

Indigo was grown under an extremely oppressive system which involved great loss to the cultivators. The planters forced the peasants to take a meagre amount as advance and enter into fraudulent contracts.[45] The planters at times would resort to a reign of terror to coerce the peasants into cultivation. Illegal confinement in factory godowns, flogging,[46] kidnapping and attacks on women and children, burning and demolition of houses were some of the methods used by the planters.[47] When cases came to the courts, the European magistrates were invariably in favour of the planters. The cultivator's land in which indigo was not cultivated was forceably brought under cultivation. The planters also lured *lathiyals*[48] (armed retainers) for the purpose. Numerous petitions to the government failed. By September 1859 the cultivators asserted their right not to grow indigo under duress. Under the leadership of Digambar Biswas and Bishnu Biswas, ex-employees of a planter, they began to organize the indigo cultivators. When a band of hundred *lathiyals* were sent to attack their village, the villagers fought back armed with their spears and *lathis*. By 1860 the disturbances flared to all the indigo growing district of Bengal. Government offices, indigo factories, the residence of the European planters were under attack. The indigo crop were also destroyed. There was unity between the ryots. The Bengal intelligentia also organized meetings and supported the revolt. Newspaper campaigns, organised meetings, memoranda and others were carried out. Din Bandhu Mitra's play, *Neel Darpan*[49] gained great fame for portraying the sufferings of the cultivators and the oppression carried out by the planters. It created great stir in Bengal. Rev. J. Long got it translated into English[50] by Michael Madhusudan Datta for which he was imprisoned for a month and fined one thousand rupees.[51]

Measures to suppress the revolt was carried out but it was not as harsh as in the case of civil rebellion or tribal uprisings. An Indigo Commission was appointed and the same pointed out the evils that was there in the system. It recommended that the oppression of the *ryots* must be stopped. With the invention of synthetic indigo in 1897, the cultivation of indigo was slowly abandoned.

In 1860–1861 troubles between the Kukis and the British came to a head. This was mainly because of the Kukis incursions into the frontier villages in the Chittagong district. In their first raid, *i.e.*, in 1860 they attacked and destroyed the village of Ramghar and then made a sudden descent on the plains of Tippera.[52] In all, around three hundred people were killed and two hundred or more were taken as prisoners.[53] In the early part of January 1861, a force of 1,250 military police under Captain Raban moved from Chittagong and entered the Kuki territory. The Kukis were intercepted and defeated, but the Kuki "problem" would continued till 1863.

About the same time another expedition was also sent against the Garos in 1861. This again came about because of the Garo raids in the Mymensingh district. Two forces of military police under Captain Morton and Lieutenant Chambers[54] carried out the expedition. The expedition was successful and the "offenders" in the Mymensingh district were arrested. It was argued that special officers should be appointed in the hills and in order to bring people into closer contacts, it was proposed that the country should be intersected with roads.[55] One road would go round the base of Garo Hills and the other right across.[56]

In Assam on the other hand, in 1861, a peasant movement broke out in Phulaguri in the Nowgong district. This was caused mainly by the ever increasing revenue extraction of the British Government. There were taxes on almost everything and whatever that was earlier procured by the Assamese peasants free of cost like timber, fish, reeds for constructing of houses and fodder for cattle were no longer free. In order to increase the market for opium, the cultivation of poppy and the indigenous production of opium was banned. The imposition of the Stamp Act in 1860 and the Income Tax and the License Tax in 1861[57] made the people doubt the real intentions of the British. These measures had much to do with the methods of re-structuring the Indian economy in the aftermath of the uprising of 1857. The ideas of James Wilson, the political economist, was applied even to British possessions in the North-East. In October 1861 the people of Phulaguri, located close to Nowgong, rose in open revolt against the unjust taxation policy of the British Indian Government.

Petitions of protest had earlier been sent to the authorities to no avail. On 17 September 1861 about 1000 peasants gathered at the Sadar Court to represent their grievances. Lieutenant Herbert Sconce, the Deputy Commissioner stood against them and detained some who had forced themselves into his room.[58] Subsequent representations were made regarding the taxes and the cultivation of poppy. A meeting was scheduled to be held on 15 October. The Deputy Commissioner sent a *daroga* with orders to disperse the crowd and to arrest the leaders; but the police failed to disperse the crowd.

On the 17th the *daroga* arrested some of the leaders but was overpowered by the mob and the leaders were freed.

On 18 October, the Deputy Commissioner believing that the situation was rather serious sent the Assistant Commissioner Lt. Singer with a party of policemen. Singer asked the people to put down their *lathies* and sticks. On their refusal, he ordered his men to take away the same. This action provoked the people and a scuffle ensued. In the midst of this, Singer was struck and fell to the ground. The police party alarmed by the situation fled from the scene. Singer was beaten to death and his body was thrown into the river Kalang.[59] News of the outbreak spread very fast and "people of Jamonamukh and Dantipur had caught the infection and a few days more might have seen it established in Jynteah".[60] The situation was saved with the timely arrival of Major Hopkinson, Agent to the Governor General, North-East Frontier on board the steamer *Lucknow* on 18 October, at Tezpur on his way to Dibrugarh. Arrangements were made and with the help of Major Campbell along with the help of the Assam Light Infantry[61] the situation was brought under control. Those who were involved in the death of Lt. Singer were arrested. The uprising at Phulaguri was a movement organised with the object of compelling the government to yield to the will of the people by the withdrawal of unpopular measures of taxation.[62]

The foregoing account will indicate the foreign rule of India by the English East India Company and later the British Crown was faced with resistance from without, as in the case of frontier tribes and those not brought under its dominion; and from within. Tribals such as those on the North-East Frontier resisted the expansion of British rule over their hills. Others who had been brought under varying degrees of subordination resisted the attempts of the Government to enforce its authority. This distinction needs to be made because resistance to alien rule did not only come from societies threatened by colonialism/imperialism.

The study of peasant movements and tribal uprisings have gained much importance today, particularly in understanding the nature of British imperialism. At first the English East

India Company being a trading body, wanted to maximise its trade by venturing into the producing areas or the villages whereby the basic structure of the Indian traditional economy was upset. The exploitation of the economy was further liberalised with the transfer of power to the British Crown by the Company after the events of 1857–1858. From this time onwards, India was thrown open not only to the Company's official but to anyone who was a subject to the British Empire. R.C. Dutt pointed out that "the empire of India was purchased by the Crown from the Company, but the people of India were charged with the purchased money. The value received by the shareholders of the Company stock was not paid by the British Crown which won an Imperial property, but was added to the Indian debt".[63] Therefore, it is primarily for this reason that the study of the uprising and rebellions which were carried out by the people after 1857 becomes more important. Such studies are not new and many scholars and historians have already dealt at length with this problems. However an analysis of the tribal problem from a historical perspective is required as not much detailed study has been made of their problems under colonial rule.

An understanding of the peasant unrest in the Indian context has been discussed briefly before we look into the case of the Jaintias. The general picture of the unrest reveals that there was a certain shift in the nature of the peasant movements after 1857. With the decline of the role of traditional rulers and leaders, the common people started to emerge as the main force in these types of movement. These gained importance all the more, when the people started to think in terms of self preservation, economic freedom and independence from foreign rule. It cannot be denied that there were instances where the fight against colonization was not the prime motive behind the revolt but the redressal of their economic problems. In the case of the Jaintias the intention of the people to fight against the forces of British imperialism was the main reason for the outbreak. The subsequent chapters and discussions will throw more light on this subject.

REFERENCES

1. Tarasankar Banerjee, *Various Bengal, Aspects of Modern History,* p. 233.
2. Ibid., p. 234.
3. Sumit Sarkar, *Modern India,* p. 44.
4. Bipan Chandra, *India's Struggle for Independence,* p. 41.
5. Ibid.
6. Ibid. The genesis of the movement in the case of the Jaintias can be related to this problem, as we shall see in the subsequent discussion.
7. Bipan Chandra, op. cit., p. 43.
8. J.N. Sarkar (ed.), *History of Bengal,* Vol. II, p. 380.
9. Sirajul Islam (ed.), *Chittagong District Records,* Vol. I, p. 239; cited in Sirajul Islam, "Tribal Resistance in Chittagong Hill Tacts (1776–1778)" in N.R. Ray (ed.), *Challenge,* p. 125.
10. Ibid.
11. N. Kaviraj, "Peasants and Adivasi Uprising (1765–1885)" in N.R. Ray (ed.), *Challenge,* p. 115.
12. Ibid., pp. 114–115.
13. K.C. Chaudhuri, *History of Modern India,* p. 435.
14. Ibid.
15. L.W. Shakespear, *The Assam Rifles,* p. 33.
16. B.P.C. No. 17, 24 November 1835; D.R. Syiemlieh, *British Administration in Meghalaya, Policy and Pattern,* pp. 46–47.
17. D.R. Syiemlieh, op. cit., p. 47; R.M. Lahiri, *Annexation of Assam,* p. 94.
18. R.M. Lahiri, op. cit., p. 114.
19. D.R. Syiemlieh, op. cit., p. 49.
20. Ibid.
21. Bipan Chandra, op. cit., p. 48; J.C. Jha, "The Kol Insurrection 1831–1832", in N.R. Ray (ed.), *Challenge,* p. 140.
22. K.K. Datta, "Santhal Insurrection", p. 34, in J.C. Jha, op. cit., p. 114.
23. Bipan Chandra, op. cit., p. 48.
24. L.W. Shakespear, op. cit., pp. 36–37.
25. Ibid.
26. L.W. Shakespear, op. cit., pp. 23–25.
27. Ibid.
28. For details see B.C. Chakravorty, *British Relations with the Hill Tribes of Assam Since 1858,* pp. 82–132.
29. V.D. Mahajan, *India Since 1526,* p. 612.
30. K.C. Chaudhuri, op. cit., p. 435.
31. Bipan Chandra, op. cit., p. 46.
32. Op. cit., p. 47.
33. Ibid.
34. Ibid.
35. Jim Masselos, *Indian Nationalism,* p. 23.
36. C. Bhattacharya, "The Bheel Rising", in N.R. Ray (ed.), *Challenge,* pp. 163–164.
37. R.C. Dutt, *The Economic History of India,* pp. 159–160.
38. P.N. Banerjee, *Indian Finance in the Days of the Company,* p. 110; cited in H.K. Barpujari, *Political History of Assam,* Vol. I, p. 88.

39. H.K. Barpujari, op. cit.
40. R.C. Kalita, "The Phulaguri Uprising of 1861: A Peasant Mass Movement", *North-East India History Association*, 10th Session, 1989, p. 311.
41. Nandini Sen, "Indigo Rebellion 1859–1861" in N.R. Ray (ed.), *Challenge*, p. 166.
42. K.C. Chaudhuri, op. cit., p. 441.
43. Nandini Sen, op. cit.
44. Ibid., see Blair Kling, *The Blue Mutiny*, for this form of exploitation.
45. C.E. Buckland, *Bengal Under the Lieutenant-Governors*, pp. 184–185; Bipan Chandra, op. cit., p. 51.
46. C.E. Buckland, op. cit., p. 185.
47. Bipan Chandra, op. cit., p. 51.
48. Ibid., K.C. Chaudhuri, op. cit., p. 442.
49. C.E. Buckland, op. cit., p. 196; Bipan Chandra, op. cit., p. 53.
50. C.E. Buckland, op. cit.
51. K.C. Chaudhuri, op. cit., p. 443.
52. C.E. Buckland, op. cit., p. 181.
53. Ibid.
54. B.C. Chakravorty, op. cit., p. 30.
55. C.E. Buckland, op. cit., p. 182.
56. B.C. Chakravorty, op.cit., p. 30.
57. R.C. Kalita, op.cit., p. 311.
58. H.K. Barpujari (Ed.), *Political History of Assam*, Vol. I, p. 90.
59. Ibid., p. 92; R.C. Kalita, op. cit., p. 317.
60. R.C. Kalita, op. cit., p. 318.
61. H.K. Barpujari, op. cit., p. 92.
62. Ibid.
63. R.C. Kalita, op. cit., p. 310.

2

Historical Background of Jaintia's Relations with the British

In order to understand the relationship between the Jaintias and the British in its fuller sense, it is necessary to look into some aspects of Jaintia history prior to the coming of the British. It is also necessary to study in what conditions the interaction between the two was made possible and what were the developments that followed, which made the British fight that "Little War"[1] in order to bring the hills under their control.

Early History: A Short Review

Originally, the Jaintia kingdom consisted of three parts viz., the Jaintia Hills; the neighbouring plains in Sylhet and territories in the present day Nowgong district. The hill portion was the original home of the ruling family.[2] In the 18th century, the kingdom was bounded in the north by Gobha-Sonapur, south by the river Surma, east by the river Kupli and in the west by the Brahmaputra. At times some principalities of Kamrup and Karimganj were included in this kingdom. The hill portion was peopled by the Jaintias, the Jaintia plains of Sylhet by the Bengali and the Nowgong portion by the Jaintias, Dimasas, Lalungs and other tribes.[3] The kingdom for that matter included both the hills and the plains and people belonging to different races have resided within it. The ruling family belonged to the Jaintia tribe. *Pnar*[4] or original people (as they claim they were the older branch or the first settlers in this region) are an offshoot of the Mon-Khmer race of South East Asia and had ascended the hills through the Assam Valley.[5] They appear to be descendants from some of the earliest Mongoloid immigrants into India who changed their languages through contact with Austric speakers, either in Burma (present Myanmar) or in the soil of India, in pre-historic times. It is likely that they were spread over a much wider tract, probably over parts at least of the plain lands of Sylhet and Kamrup, before they became finally confined to the hills.[6]

Before the evolution of the institution of kingship or monarchy in Jaintia hills, there were a number of independent villages each under the control of the *Langdoh* (priest) who wielded power from the people. The priest exercised, besides his religious functions, civil and criminal function as well. The *Langdoh* was at one time both the sacred and secular chief of the Jaintias.[7] The process of polity formation among the Jaintias started with the development of village or *Chnong* consisting of groups of families belonging to different clans or *Kurs*.[8] A group of villages formed a *Raid* council and a group of *Raids* formed an *Elaka* under a *Daloi*. The *Elakas* on the other hand formed a confederation which gave rise to the formation of a *Hima* or state which was headed by the *Syiem*.[9]

With the conquest of the Jaintia plains in the 13th century,[10] the *Syiem* had direct access to the plains areas and the people of the plains addressed him as the *Rajah*. In the hills he was referred to as *Syiem* and thereby performing a dual role in the process. No other chief in the region had enjoyed this dual status. Along with this a three tier system of administration was established in the Jaintia *Hima*. The first tier was that of the *Syiem*, the second tier were the institutions of the *Raids* or *Elakas* or provinces under the *Daloi* and the third was the village administration each under the village headman (*U Waheh Chnong*).[11]

The contact with the plains brought about significant changes in the political, economic and social life of the Jaintias.[12] The plain areas as stated earlier was predominantly inhabited by the Bengali Hindus and Muslims whose main occupation was agriculture. These people had taken to extensive agricultural works where most of the jungle land was brought under cultivation. It was during this time that Hinduism had started to have an impact in the Jaintia kingdom.[13] Hinduism posing as an organised religion, having clearly defined doctrines and a large number of followers attracted the attention of the *Syiem* and his followers. The *Raja* of Jaintia and the members of his family were soon converted to Hinduism, and they formed a distinct community in the capital of the kingdom.[14] The capital of the kingdom was at Jaintiapur in the Surma Valley. The capital town also known as 'Nijpat', bore the stamp of prosperity that the state had attained.[15] A detail description of the place was given by S.M. Ali. He writes:[16]

> Nijpat was bounded on the North and West by Noyagang, on the East by Nageraticherra and on the' South by Bargang. The town was encircled by deep moat to protect it from invasion. There were three gateways leading to the town which were guarded by soldiers. There were a fort and a pair of cannons in each gateway. The dimension of the cannons are: length 9 ft. 2 diameter of the bore 3 ft. Similar cannons are to be seen at Mynkyrdam and Kyndiar in Khyrim state. These had been captured by Siem of Nonkrem from Jaintia Raja. Two of these cannons are removed to Sylhet. Two cannons near the southern gateway of Nijpat are still to be seen. The city was divided into 39 mahallas and each mahalla was called by a hati name ending with hati, para, bari or nagar such as Mahut, Darji, Hati, Natpara, Baviapara etc. The population of the city at the time of annexation is said to have been 26000.
>
> The royal palace was erected on a hillock about 40 cubits high and was surrounded by walls which were 7 cubits in height. The principal gateway of the palace was to the south. There are 14 stone steps leading to this gateway. The royal palace was divided into three parts, the outermost of which was allotted for the accommodation of the subordinate chieftains when on a visit to the capital.

The Author continues

> The old palace was situated in the site of the present Jaintiapur thana and inspection bungalow. It was used as his residence by Fateh Khan after the new palace had been erected. The temple of Jayanteswari was situated to the south of the old palace. The temple was surrounded by wall which were 8 cubits high and had engravings of wild animals etc. on them. The remnants of the walls are still to be seen. The idol of Jyateswari was stolen in 1900.
>
> South of the temple was the Darbar Hall of the king. There were stone seats for the chieftains and notables in the hall. These seats are still to be seen. South of the Darbar hall was a high monument known as Bardeul. The whole of Nijpat could be seen from its top. Signals used to be given from it in times of emergency. It had been built during the reign of Bar Gosain II. Its ruins are still to be seen.

An interesting account of the Jaintia Raj was also given by the English officers and military personnel stationed in the hills from time to time. Among the early English administrators, Robert Lindsay, Collector of Sylhet had left a delightful account about the Jaintia *Raja* and his *Raj*. He writes in his memoir.[17]

> The Jointah Rajah, of the Cusseah tribe, was my nearest frontier neighbour; he was by far the most powerful and the most civilized of the whole, holding large possessions both in the mountain and the plain, about fifty miles distant ... he requested me to accompany him to his barge to partake of the *shekar* or hunting party, previously prepared for our amusement.

In the hills, Nartiang was the summer capital of the king and was the principal centre of Hindu worship and a Hindu temple attributed to goddess Kali and Shiv was constructed. By 1828 it was observed that "within the last half a century, the Brahmanical doctrines have made such progress, that most of the leading men, have adopted them and have been classed by their spiritual instructors in the Khetri or military tribe.[18]

The extension of the Jaintia Raj, both in the north and in the south of the hills had greatly influenced the Jaintias to adopt the agricultural practices which were carried out in those areas. The Jaintias were among the first hill tribes of North-East India to have taken to sedentary cultivation as a viable agricultural practice.[19] They were skilled wet rice cultivators.[20]

As to their trade, the people would visit Sylhet and Jaintiapur. There was an extensive network of trade through this route. The main items of trade were rice, salt, tobacco, cotton, iron ore, wax, ivory, betel-leaf, cloth etc.[21] The Jaintia rulers were also known to have issued coins called *Kattra taka*[22] but which had limited circulation. They served more as a symbol of status than as a medium of exchange, thereby implying the independence of the issuing authority.[23]

Initial Contact with the English

The contact between the Jaintias and the English can be traced back to the 18th century. According to the oral tradition, the people would make use of the navigable rivers to frequent the frontiers of Eastern Bengal and at times reach Calcutta in pursuit of their trade and commerce.[24] Trade and commerce had brought these people into contact with the English East India Company and other Europeans long before the granting of the *Diwani* by the Mughal Emperor Shah Alam II in 1765. The granting of the *Diwani* and the subsequent control of Sylhet district by the English East India Company by 1770 made the contacts between the Company's official and the Jaintias more frequent.[25] This was made possible because of the geographical extension of the Jaintia kingdom into the Bengal plains.

With time it was noticed that the interest that the Company was showing in trade and the influences which its merchants were having on the other tribes sent strong signals of resentment to the Jaintias. This was mainly because of the apprehension that their trade and commerce with Bengal would be jeopardised.[26] The interest of the Company's merchants to carry out trade in limestone by signing treaties with the Khasi chiefs and the dispute over the Satbak *parganas* within the Jaintia kingdom, which the Company officials wanted to occupy, caused misunderstanding and friction between the Jaintias and the Company officials. Since the trade in limestone was profitable, the Company merchants were determined to continue with this trade. The competition which the Jaintias were facing from these organised form of merchantilism was a clear threat to their trade and commerce that they had carried out from early days. As the Jaintia kingdom included the portion of the plains of Sylhet the trade the river Surma was under Raja Chatra Sing's supervision, *i.e.*, the portion that fell under his territory. The Jaintia Raja would collect taxes from these boats plying through his territory. Since the English East India Company was carrying its trade through those areas, a free passage down the river Surma was essential.[27] It was stated by the Company officials that the Raja "time and again, obstructed the Company's boats as they passed down to Dacca, exacting tolls, looting their contents and causing them endless delays and annoyance".[28] It was also asserted that the Raja "had committed many incursions upon the lands from which the Company drew its revenue, seriously affecting the returns."[29] It is generally concluded that the expedition that was carried out by Ellerker in 1774 was an assertion of the Company to control this waterway. To this it may be mentioned that since the English East India Company was essentially a trading company and maximization of profits was its prime objective, a need for "free passage down the river Surma"[30] was essential in their economic interest.

Military Expedition

Sylhet was then under the charge of William Thackeray. He reported the state of affairs to the Calcutta and urged that measures should be adopted. Nothing but active military operations would prove effective in this case and at this the authorities at Calcutta hesitated. The authorities felt that not only was there a question of expense but there was still the dislike of resorting to arms if it could be avoided. In the case of the Jaintia Raja, it was held that the only satisfactory conclusion to a military expedition against him appeared to be the acquisition of his territory.[31] This was not the policy of the Company government or of the Court of Directors in

England. It was further argued that an expedition and the acquisition of the territory could only increase the responsibilities of the Company for the protection of the frontiers and this did not at all appeal to the authorities at Calcutta whose hands during this time were more than full with other Indian problems.

On 22 July, 1773, orders were passed to attach Sylhet to the Dacca district and Thackeray was directed to make over charge to Richard Barwell and return to his seat at the Dacca Council, but for over a year these orders remained a dead letter and though they were more than once repeated, Thackeray waved them aside. It was owing to the need of his presence during the Jaintia expedition, that he was so long allowed to disregard the order for his repeated representations had at last had weight, and the expedition, though on a small scale, was decided upon. At this repeated and particular instance, Richard Barwell, who was the Chief of the Dacca Council finally wrote to Thackeray on 8 February, 1774, that he had directed Ensign Leake, who was on a visit to Dacca, to join him with fifty men of the Dacca militia, and to put himself at the head of the troops stationed in Sylhet. Ensign Leake was put under Thackeray's orders and was directed to follow such instructions as the latter should think fit to issue to him.[32] This was how the English East India Company sent their first military expedition into a state situated in North-East India.

The steps taken by Richard Barwell appears to have been extremely bold and fearful of being considered to have exceeded his powers, he wrote apologetically to the Board two days after issuing them:

> You will perceive by the public letters despatched hence tonight that I have been led into an irregularity from the urgency of the occasion that called for an officer to lead the force now in Sylhet for the defence of the province, requesting either Ensign Leake might be officially approved to lead the expedition or another officer appointed in his place.

He added that "the conduct of the Jaintia Raja I make no doubt you will think merits chastisement",[33] urging that the

Raja should be made to give satisfaction for the depredations he had committed by reimbursing the expense of the troops and paying an equivalent for the damage that he had done. The force already despatched to Sylhet, small as it was, Barwell thought, would be enough to effect the submission of the Raja, and he further suggested that the territory between the foot of the hills and the river Surma should be taken possession of.[34] No elaborate explanation was given on the excesses that were carried out by the Raja as claimed by Richard Barwell which necessitated the despatching of troops.

The Board sticking to its policies suggested that the Raja should be brought to reason and to pay compensation to the damage he had done, but at the same time allowed Ensign Leake to retain on duty in Sylhet, and the task of carrying out the understanding with the Raja was left to Captain Ellerker of the 7th Battalion of *sepoys*. He was appointed to command the expedition with a detachment of his battalion consisting of three companies.[35] How little prepared for resistance in case of attack the English factories were in those days was everywhere in evidence. At the first outbreak, a young officer who happened to be in Dacca was apparently the only officer available to lead the few troops that could be spared to Sylhet, while Captain Ellerker's first request for troops and fifty barrels of ball cartridges, was met by Richard Barwell's reply from Dacca—'I do not believe there is in store above two thousand ball cartridges. Whatever there is, shall be immediately despatched and a further quantity as soon as prepared, shall be forwarded to you, but as that further supply must be made up with country powder in the garrison, you will probably be able to supply yourself full as well at Sylhet. However, lest you might not, the supply shall be sent to you'.[36]

On 24th March, 1774, Captain Ellerker and his *sepoys* took control over Rajagunge, a place which was only six miles from the Raja's capital, but after a stiff resistance by the people of that area, the advanced guard of Ellerker was attacked and in the process two *sepoys* were wounded.[37] The rugged nature of the country and the fear of surprise attacks by the Jaintias, who had the advantage of knowing the land said much on the moral of the *sepoys* that Ellerker was heading. When the troops arrived on the close to Rajagunge they found that the Jaintias had established themselves in a fortified position with trenches more formidable than what the Company's force had anticipated.[38] Ellerker managed to disperse them, but not without losing a *sepoy*.[39] Ellerker's advance was checked for two days because of incessant rain. The following morning, the Rajah sent a messenger telling Ellerker not to advance further until he was informed with the demands of the Company. In the meantime preparations were made by the Jaintia Raja for a surprise attack on the Company's troops.[40] Around three o'clock in the afternoon a large number of people and herds of elephants surrounded the *sepoys* camp and attacked it from every side. The troops retaliated and after a long struggle the troops managed to disperse the Jaintias who disappeared into the jungles.[41] Ellerker advanced and took possession of Jaintiapur, while the Raja Chatra Sing moved to the hills near Borkhat. By 3rd August a considerable number of people had submitted to the Company and the proposal of annexing the whole of the flat country to Sylhet was made by Thackeray.[42] The civil officer also realised that his proposal would meet with success only if the area promised revenue. The other reason for his stress of annexing the plain tracts of the Jaintia Raja was to set an example to other chiefs in the hills as a consequence of meddling with his district.[43]

Its Aftermath

Richard Barwell received the news of the success of the expedition at Dacca, but was placed in a very difficult position. There were three options open to the Company: firstly, to take possessions of the Raja's land; secondly, to hand the land over to another chieftain, who would be friendly to the Company; thirdly, to restore the Raja on his furnishing guarantees for his future good behaviour.[44] Interestingly, the authorities at Dacca were torn between their desire to punish the Jaintia Raja and their intense aversion to acquire his territory. Richard Barwell was in favour of restoring it to the Raja. The reason for this was that it was unreasonable on their part to annex it as the tract had been under the possession of the Raja's family for a long time. This could be done only if the Raja showed signs of coming to terms[45] with the English East

India Company. The other alternative was to transfer the Raja's land to Ahmmed Riza the *thannadar* of Pandua, in order to avoid the expense of military establishment for its defence. The idea was conveyed to the then Governor-General, Warren Hasting who was not very impressed by the arguments of the Dacca Council. It may be recalled that the English East India Company was a trading body and profits were necessarily its first consideration. The Raja's land, on the other hand, did not yield much so as to meet the expenses of the government. The authorities in Calcutta were alarmed at the expenditure involved in the expedition and the official instructions to Thackeray was to settle the affairs quickly and to avoid all possible expense.

As the hot weather advanced a settlement with the Jaintia Raja appeared to be imminent. The authorities in Calcutta had also expressed itself in favour of the restoration of the Raja in preference to the plan proposed by the officials of Dacca. On 12 June, 1774, Ellerker returned to Sylhet, but before that a settlement with the Jaintia Raja was carried out before he was restored. The important terms that were concluded with the Raja were as follows:[46]

a) The Raja was to pay Rs. 15,000 as compensation for the cost of the expedition.
b) There was to be free and undisturbed navigation along the Surma river.
c) The Raja was not to interfere with the activities of the Company.
d) As a pledge, one of his nearest relation was handed over to Thackeray.

Chatra Sing died on 18 June, 1774, and the terms of compromise with the Raja was confirmed by the Board of Directors on the 28th of the same month. Chatra Sing was succeeded by his nephew Jatranarayan.[47] The news of these developments were conveyed to the authorities in Dacca by Thackeray. The Jaintia expedition ended and the young Raja carried out his reign over the territory that he had inherited. From 1774 to 1778, Jatranarayan carried out his reign peacefully and there was no further intervention whatsoever on the part of the Company officials on that matter; but this was not to remain for long. In 1779, it was alleged, that some people who were subjects of the Raja carried out depredations in the British territory. Accordingly, *havildar* Biswanath and ten *sepoys* were sent to assist the Raja to nab the people responsible for the act.[48] It appears that this small contingent was enough to subdue those who have carried out those depredations; but the *havildar* did not return without carrying out excesses. The Raja complained the matter to the Collector Robert Lindsay of the irregularities that were committed. The matter was taken up by Lindsay and the *vakil* of the Raja who was assulted was also summoned. The *havildar* was sent to Dacca for a trial by court martial.[49]

Between 1779 down to 1820, there were no instances that would make interference from the East India Company side necessary. In 1821, it was reported that three Jaintias subject were caught in Sylhet district while attempting to kidnap a person from the Company territory.[50] The three were tried and on examination it appeared that they were sent by Chun Rungbot the brother-in-law of the late Ram Sing.[51] By this time Ram Sing II was the ruler of the Jaintias. The Company government gave a serious warning to the Raja reminding him that in the event of another instance the offender would be publicly put to death and that if the demand for the surrender of the individual in question were not complied, the government would consider that the Raja had taken the guilt upon himself and would proceed against him accordingly.[52] After this warning the Jaintias made no attempt to carry off human victims for sacrifices for some years.[53]

Defence Alliance

In 1824, the First Anglo-Burmese war broke out. During the course of the war, Ava threatened to over-run Jaintia. The Burmese Commander-in-Chief of Assam in his communication to the Jaintia Raja demanded the latter's submission to the Burmese King and that the Raja should proceed by land, for the purpose of placing him on the *musnud*.[54] The Raja on seeing the threat to his kingdom entered into a treaty of alliance with the Company in 1824, under the provisions of which he was exempted from the payments of any tribute.[55] It was only after the signing of the treaty with the Raja that the British authority reacted strongly to the intentions of the Burmese over Jaintia. The Agent to the Governor General, David Scott, wrote a letter to the Commander of the Burmese forces at Cachar, Mahanund Kegooteen, in the following words:[56]

> And it appears that you write, that the old friendship subsisting between us and your Rajah is at an end, and that war will ensue. Of the result of the hostilities, we have no apprehension but we shall request to find the long established friendship between the two countries uninterrupted by your proceedings. Hitherto you have experienced the advantages of being at peace with us, now if you insist upon war, you will also taste its bitter fruit.

As far as Jaintia was concerned, the letter had this to say:[57]

> Now I hear that you design to enter the Jynteah country and that you have sent people to the Rajah. Therefore, I acquaint you that we will not permit the execution of this act of aggression. First, because the Rajah's ancestor received that country as a gift after conquest from the Honourable Company and he himself has sought our protection. Second, because, as you openly threatened war, we cannot permit you to occupy that or any other favourable position for commencing hostilities.

The understanding between the Raja Ram Sing II and David Scott, the Governor General's Agent was such that the Raja was promised assistance of Government troops if his own resources were actively employed in repulsing the enemy and threatened with punishment if he admitted the Burmese.[58] The *Syiem* gave valuable assistance to the David Scott and the Company troops by giving a free passage through his territory during their march from Sylhet to Assam. David Scott was happy with the help he obtained from the Raja during the war.[59] The Raja had collected a force which was said to consist of several thousand archers[60] and had undoubtedly the means of defending his own territory.[61] The Anglo-Burmese war came to an end in 1826 with one of the terms of the treaty of Yandaboo, February 1826, being the renunciation of Jaintia by the Burmese.[62] It appears however, that by this time the Raja had become entirely dependant on the protection of the East India Company government.[63]

Kidnapping Incidents

In 1827, the case of kidnapping another of Company subject was reported from Sylhet and the magistrate was requested to submit a report in order to study how far such "practices are countenanced by the Rajah or by persons acting under his authority."[64] During this time the relationship between the Raja and the Company's officials had deteriorated. Robertson who had succeeded David Scott as the Agent to the Governor General, charged the Raja for not fulfilling his obligation in the late war. The *Raja* was also charged of capturing considerable tracts in Assam and had also established a *chokey* at Chapparmookh.[65] To top it all the Government was annoyed with the continued prevalence of human sacrifice in the kingdom where the Company's subjects were waylaid to be immolated.

The already strained relationship took a serious turn in 1832, when two Company's subjects who were passing along the highroad in Assam were suddenly seized, carried up into the hills in the neighbourhood of Gobha and after having being decked with new clothes and jewels, were led away to be sacrificed together with two other persons. One of them succeeded in making his escape and reported the incident to the authorities. As far as the other three were concerned they were never heard of again.[66] They were said to have been sacrificed in the temple of Kali within Gobha territory. The man who was responsible for this deed was said to be the ex-*Raja* of Gobha, Chatra,[67] who was a vassal of the *Raja* of Jaintia.[68] Correspondence were carried out between the Company's official and the Raja on the matter of human sacrifice and the latter was reminded of the consequences and warnings given before about the refusal of surrendering the guilty persons. The tradition in Jaintia refers to a certain *mantri* of Nijpat (Jaintiapur) who had been imprisoned by the *Raja* and who in order to take revenge on the Raja invented the story of kidnapping of Company's subject.[69] *Raja* Ram Sing II assured the authorities of looking into the matter and while the matter was under correspondence the *Raja* died on the 25 of September, 1832. Ram Sing II was succeeded by his grand nephew Rajendra Sing, a young lad of seventeen years.[70]

Meanwhile in the British camp discussions were carried out about the fate of the Jaintia kingdom. Captain Fisher, Superintendent of Cachar, who had intimate knowledge of the region, pointed out in a letter to Francis Jenkins, Agent to the Governor-General North-East India, the mistake of David Scott of not realising any tribute from the Raja of Jaintia.[71] Robertson earlier, on the other hand, in reporting about the accession of the young ruler took it as an opportunity for the revision of the Treaty, which according to him, without the Company's support the *Raja* would have been unable to maintain himself even for a year.[72] It was estimated that the *Raja's* territory in Sylhet and Assam which were considered to be fertile plains could yield a revenue of one lakh and fifty thousand rupees per annum. Robertson recommended that a sum of rupees ten thousand be exacted as an annual tribute from the new *Raja*,[73] and that recognition to him should be made depending on his agreeing to pay the tribute.[74] The problem for the Raja was such that his subjects made all their contributions in kind. In this regard, Robertson proposed that a system of taxation should be introduced in the *Raja's* territory in order to meet the demands.[75] According to the traditional custom the *Raja* had no right to agree to the recommendations without discussing the same with the *Dalois*, the head of the administrative divisions of which the state of Jaintia was composed and of which the *Raja* was merely the head.[76] The *Raja* therefore asked for some time to discuss the matter with the *Dalois*, but Robertson was for an immediate answer. In a meeting that was held at Sylhet, on 21 May, 1833, Robertson was so indignant that not only was the *Raja* denied customary honours due to a prince, but he was told that he could be recognised only as a relation of the late *Raja*, who is taking temporary charge of the country. In other words, as a mere *Jemedar* or custodian and not as a *Raja* of Jaintia. What was humiliating was the manner in which the *Raja* was dismissed from the meeting unceremoniously without giving him the right of salute from the guards of honour in attendance.[77]

The *Raja* wrote to the officiating Governor-General Sir Charles Metcalfe about the humiliating treatment and about his inability of paying the tribute stating in his petition that the country of Jaintia was very small and that the larger part of it was composed of hills. He appealed for tolerant treatment,[78] but the Governor-General was in favour of the proposal made by Robertson. He wanted the *Raja* to contribute towards the general defence of the frontier, and also informed him that the treaty signed earlier was a personal one and hence required amendment.[79] The Court of Directors of the Government of Bengal on the other hand disagreed with the above views and expressed their displeasure at the attempts to force a tribute on the *Raja*, but this had no effect.[80]

To add to his miseries, the *Raja* was at that time facing another problem from a different quarter altogether. It came from the *Daloi* of Nartiang who wanted to depose the *Raja* when the latter was showing signs of favour to his rival the *Daloi* of Jowai. The *Daloi* of Nartiang was encouraged all the more when he came to know that Robertson refused to recognise Rajendra Sing as the *Raja* of Jaintia.[81] The question of paying tributes having not been solved and embarrassment caused by defection among the *Dalois* that the question of human sacrifice gained importance once again. The *Daloi* of Nartiang asserted that Sobha Sing, the chief of Gobha carried out the human sacrifice under the orders of the heir apparent, Rajendra Sing. He further added that, Chatra Sing who was imprisoned by the late Ram Sing had nothing to do with the sacrifice. Robertson without cross-checking the information came to the conclusion that the Raja of Jaintia was sheltering Sobha Sing and requested the government to punish Rajendra Sing for the non-delivery of the chief of Gobha and others who have committed the crime. Robertson further added that Rajendra Sing was a promoter of human sacrifice, but this again was not proved by the former.[82] It was during this period, early 1834, that Robertson was relieved by Francis Jenkins.

On coming to office, Francis Jenkins held a thorough enquiry into the case of Ram Sing II. The enquiry led to interesting revelations. He discovered that Sobha Sing was totally ignorant of the whole transaction and therefore was released by Jenkins. The person for whom he was mistaken was the ex-*Raja* Chatra Sing, the predecessors of Sobha Sing who was still in confinement.[83] Jenkins concluded that "the result of this enquiry has not in my opinion legally convicted anyone said to have been concerned."[84] In these circumstances, Jenkins seemed to have hesitated to take the responsibility of pronouncing a verdict of guilty on the *Raja*, but the Government thought otherwise. They held the *Raja* responsible for the cruel incident and therefore believed must be punished.[85] His plains territories in Sylhet and Assam would be taken away and only the hill territories would remain with him. While these discussions were going on, Rajendra Sing in the month of August, 1834 apprehended four of the offenders so long demanded by the Company authorities and handed them over. In a letter addressed to the Political Department Captain Jenkins admitted the surrender of the offenders, a fact which had been totally overlooked by Edward Gait who holds the non-delivery of the criminals to be the sole cause of the annexation of the territory of the Raja.[86] Interestingly, in the letter written by the Governor-General, Lord William Bentinck to Rajendra Sing, nothing was mentioned about the surrendering of the offenders by the Raja. He wrote:[87]

> In the year 1821, three persons, subjects of your Government were seized in the Sylhet District while in the act of dragging away a young man, and on their examination it appeared they had been sent by Oo Chun Rungbat Koonwar, brother-in-law of your late father, to seize a man for the purpose of offering him up as a sacrifice to the shrine of Kali; and that they were endeavoring to carry this abominable purpose into effect when they were seized by the villagers and delivered over to the civil authorities. The men were tried, convicted and punished, and an intimation was made to your late father to the effect that, if another instance should occur of a British subject being kidnapped for a similar purpose. His lordship would immediately demand the surrender of the individuals at whose instigation the crime might have been committed, and that on proof of their having been instigators of the

> attempt, such individuals, however high in rank, would be publicly put to death, and that if the demand for the surrender of the individual in question were not complied with, the Governor General in Council would consider the Rajah as having taken the guilt upon himself and would proceed against him accordingly. Again in the year 1832, two British subjects were passing along the high road in Assam when they were suddenly seized, carried up into the hills in the neighbourhood of Goba, and after having been decked with new clothes and jewels they were led away to be sacrificed, together with two other persons, also subjects of this government. One of the individuals first named succeeded in making his escape, and on his return to the plains he gave information of what had occurred, and, as his statement was corroborated by many collateral circumstances, there is no reason whatever to doubt the truth of what he said. The crime was perpetuated, it is to be feared, as regard the other three individuals, as they have never since been heard of.
>
> Since this period you have been repeatedly required by my Agent in Assam to surrender the guilty individuals, but all to no purpose, and there is even strong reason to suspect that you have not only wilfully screened the perpetrators of this horrible crime, but that you were cognizant of it yourself while you were yet heir apparent during your father's life time. Your possession in the plains are confiscated and that those in the hills would be so likewise if such crime occurred therein hereafter.

It is still not apparent as to the charges that were levelled against the *Raja*, but for some reason or the other the authorities had decided to take strong measures that would go against the interest of the *Raja*. It appears that their differences regarding boundary between Jaintia and Assam along the banks of the Kupli river and the *chokey* that was established right from the time of Ram Sing at Chappermookh for levying tolls on all goods passing through this *ghat* had much to say. These areas came under the control of Ram Sing when he decided to assist in the war which broke out in Assam between the Company's troops and those of the king of Ava, where the Jaintia king would move with a force and attack the enemy "to the east of Guwahati". The Company had agreed upon the conquest of Assam and therefore, conferred upon the Raja a part of that territory proportionate to the extent of his exertions in the common cause.[88] As far as the case of *chokey* was concerned, it was reported that the Collectors of the *Raja* carried out extortions which sometimes led to violence. Earlier, David Scott had requested Ram Sing II to remove the *chokey* but nothing was settled. The correspondence was carried out by the successors of Scott and Ram Sing, but there was no tangible result. A bone of contention remained over this issue. The encroachment on the plains of Assam, refusal to pay tributes and the practices of human sacrifices were the charges that were levelled against the *Raja*, which again was not proved.

Annexation

After the surrendering of the offenders in the month of August 1834, it seemed that the English authorities were satisfied with their main demands and for the next six months there was no significant developments that would unsettle the relationship between the two governments. On 15th March, 1835, under the instruction of the Government, Captain Lister, commanding the Sylhet Light Infantry Battalion, in company with H. Inglis, then having local rank in the same corps, proceeded to Jaintiapur with a strong detachment.[89] The two seized the whole of the *Raja's* property, real and personal in the plains to the value of about a lakh and a half rupees, apparently even including his clothes and cooking pots.[90] This came as a big surprise to Rajendra Sing for no warning had been given at any time to the *Raja*. The reason put forward for this act of intrusion was the non-delivery of the offenders implicated in the atrocities of Gobha and the participation of the king himself in those acts; charges that were not proved. The act of taking away the personal belonging of the *Raja* was regarded to be a severe measure and Lister was directed by the authorities to restore back everything except arms, ammunition or otherwise.[91] The *Raja* did not resist and was captured. Jaintiapur was captured and occupied by the

Company's troops on 16 March 1835. The annexation of the territory was made known through a proclamation.[92] After the capture of the *Raja,* the Jaintia people wanted to resist the English but were prevented from doing so by the *Raja.* The *Raja* was given the option of retaining his property in the hills, but the *Raja* refused the offer "stating his inability to manage it".[93] A pension of Rs. 500 per month was assigned to the *Raja* for his support and he was directed to reside at Sylhet.[94] The act of dismissing the *Raja* and seizure of his property was looked upon by the hill people as an act of treachery. The pleas on which Jaintia was annexed was not well grounded and in any case it appears to have been a break of the Treaty executed between Ram Sing and David Scott.[95]

The annexation of the plain territories of the Jaintia kingdom meant the extinction of the same as the hill territories were subsequently surrendered by the *Raja.* The main reason for this withdrawal on the part of the *Raja* was that the hills had not the enormous resources to afford him support. Further still the Raja was not confident of the support that he would get from the powerful *Dalois* of the hills such as Nartiang and Jowai.[96]

Dissatisfaction in the Hills

Five months after the annexation of the Jaintia kingdom Lister decided to move again towards the hills with a contingent. There was no reason given for this act. Earlier there were reports that the people of Jowai and the neighbouring areas had planned to attack the plains of Sylhet to drive away the Company's people and to retrieve back those territories which they had lost. When Lister made this move into the hills, he was attacked. Lister was able to occupy Jowai and held out a threat of burning the other villages if the chiefs did not surrender. It was just a matter of time before the chiefs surrendered themselves and Lister left the Jaintia Hills, leaving behind a small force as a token of the establishment of the Government claim to the hills.[97] To this development, a historian comments:[98]

> In this way the whole of Jaintia kingdom was annexed over very trivial issues that had no justification. Whereas the Khasi states existence was tolerated even after their resistance, Jaintia was made to yield to British rule. The Jaintia reaction was insignificant at this stage. Twenty five years later their resentment to British rule was expressed in rebellion.

He further adds "it was wrongly conceived that Jaintia Hills formed part of the Khasi hills".[99] The Act VI of 1835 provided for the judicial control of the Khasi hills and Jaintia hills.[100] Realizing the anomaly that the British were not in control of Jaintia when the Act was passed, Act XXI of 1836 subsequently sanctioned the general annexation of the entire Jaintia kingdom to Sylhet and the extension to it of the laws and regulations in force in Bengal. It was only the plains portion of the *Jaintia* Hills adjoining Sylhet that was brought under the operation of this order.[101] No orders for retaining the hill areas under Lister's superintendence can be traced and Lister himself could find no instruction on the subject.[102]

From the above it appears that the Hills were placed in a very anonymous position. Perhaps this is one reason to explain as to why there was hardly any control over the Jaintia Hills by the authorities from their Cherrapunji headquarters. The administration in the hills was carried out by the *Dalois* and their assistants with little or no interference from the Company's authorities.

REFERENCES

1. *The Friend of India,* March 5, 1863.
2. S.M. Ali, *The History of Jaintia,* p. 1.
3. J.B. Bhattacharjee, "Brahmanical Myths, Royal Legitimation and the Jaintia State Formation" in *North-Eastern Hill University Journal of Social Sciences and Humanities,* Vol. 3, No. 1, p. 47; also in J.B. Bhattacharjee, *Social and Polity Formation in Pre-Colonial North-East India,* p. 79; S.M. Ali, op. cit., pp. 4–5; R.M. Lahiri, *The Annexation of Assam,* pp. 151–157.
4. Preference is given to this term, especially to those settlers who have spread themselves in the central upland region by which the people prefer to be identified. They were also called Syntengs or Jaintias. For this study, Jaintia will be preferred as it is a generic term.

5. J.B. Bhattacharjee, "Brahmanical Myths, Royal Legitimation and the Jaintia Formation" in *North-Eastern Hill University Journal of Social Sciences and Humanities*, Vol. 3, No. 1, p. 47.
6. P.K. Das, Gupta, *Life and Culture of Matrilineal Tribes of Meghalaya*, p. 7.
7. B. Pakem, "Social and Political Institutions of the Jaintias of Meghalaya" in Jayanta Sarkar and B. Dutta Ray, *Social and Political Institutions of the Hill People of North-East India*, p. 90.
8. J.B. Bhattacharjee, op. cit., p. 47. op. cit., p. 81.
9. Ibid.
10. B. Pakem, op. cit., p. 81.
11. N.C. Shadap-Sen, *The Origin and Early History of the Khasi-Synteng People*, pp. 200–202; also B. Pakem, op. cit., p. 81.
12. Shobhan N. Lamare, "The Cultural Transition of the Pnars" (M.Phil unpublished dissertation), p. 56.
13. Ibid.
14. S.M. Ali, op. cit., p. 72.
15. J.B. Bhattacharjee, op. cit., p. 53.
16. S.M. Ali, op. cit., pp. 75–77; J.B. Bhattacharjee, op. cit., p. 53.
17. Robert Lindsay, "Anecdotes of an Indian Life" in *Lives of the Lindsays*, pp. 181–184.
18. P.N. Dutta, *Impact of the West on the Khasis and Jaintias*, p. 9.
19. Shobhan N. Lamare, op. cit., p. 50.
20. Ibid.
21. According to oral tradition, trade on these were mainly carried out through barter or cowries.
22. Vasant Chowdhury and Parimal Ray, "Some New and Rare Coins from the Old Hindu Kingdom of Jayantipur" in Jai Prakash Singh and Nissar Ahmad (ed.) *Coinage and Economy of North-Eastern States of India*, p. 31; Nissar Ahmad, "The Jayantiya Coins", op. cit., p. 46; P.N. Dutta, *Impact of the West on the Khasis and Jaintias*, p. 1, also in L.S. Gassah, "Trade Routes and Trade Relations Between Jaintia Hills and Sylhet District in the Pre-Independence Period" in the *Proceedings of North-East India History Association*, 9th Session, pp. 485–489.
23. Shobhan, N. Lamare, op. cit., p. 52; J.P. Singh, "Jaintia Coins and the Koch Historical Tradition: An Examination" in N.I. Bulletin, *Numismatics International*, Vol. 22, No. 5, May 1988, p. 112; A.N. Lahiri, "A Unique Gold Coin of the time of Bada Gosain II of Jayantipur" in J.P. Singh and Nissar Ahmad (ed.), op. cit., pp. 28–29.
24. P.M. Passah, "The First Two Anglo-Jaintia Wars" in *Proceedings of North-East India History Association*, 13th Session, 1993, p. 225.
25. Ibid.
26. Ibid.
27. S.B. Bradley-Birt, *Sylhet Thackeray*, p. 154.
28. Ibid.
29. Ibid.
30. Ibid.
31. S.B. Bradley-Birt, *Sylhet Thackeray*, p. 155.
32. Op. cit., p. 157.
33. Ibid.

34. Op. cit., p. 158.
35. Op. cit., p. 159.
36. Op. cit., p. 160.
37. S.M. Ali, *The History of Jaintia*, pp. 44–45; S.B. Bradley-Birt, op. cit., p. 161.
38. S.M. Ali, op. cit., p. 45; S.B. Bradley-Birt, op. cit., p. 162.
39. S.M. Ali, op. cit., p. 45.
40. Ibid.
41. S.B. Bradley-Birt, op. cit., p. 164.
42. Ibid., p. 165.
43. Ibid., pp. 165–166.
44. Ibid., p. 166.
45. Ibid., p. 167.
46. S.M. Ali, op. cit., p. 46; S.B. Bradley-Birt, op. cit., p. 164.
47. S.M. Ali, op. cit., p. 47.
48. Ibid.
49. S.M. Ali, op. cit., p. 51; *Sylhet District Records*, Vol. I, p. 92.
50. R.B. Pemberton, *Report on the Eastern Frontier of British India*, p. 219; Alexander Mackenzie, *The North-East Frontier of India*, p. 217; also S.M. Ali, *The History of Jaintia*, p. 55.
51. Home Public No. 30 C; 3 July 1863, J.C. Haughton to the Secretary Government of Bengal; S.M. Ali, op. cit., p. 55.
52. Home Public, op. cit.
53. P.N. Dutta, *Impact of the West on the Khasis and Jaintias*, p. 79.
54. H.H. Wilson, No. 23(c) June 1824, *Documents Illustration of the Burmese War*, from the Government Gazette, p. 21.
55. P.N. Dutta, op. cit., p. 79.
56. H.H. Wilson, Documents No. 28, 23 February 1824, Extract from a Despatch from the Governor General in Council to the Select Committee of the Court of Directors, p. 31.
57. Ibid.
58. S.M. Ali, *The History of Jaintia*, p. 56.
59. R.B. Pemberton, op. cit., p. 220; P.N. Dutta, op. cit., p. 79.
60. S.M. Ali, op. cit., p. 56.
61. David Scott *Memoirs*, Calcutta 1832, Extract from a letter from David Scott to G. Swinton, Secretary, Budderpore, 3 February 1824, p. 74.
62. E.A. Gait, *History of Assam*, pp. 340–341.
63. P.N. Dutta, op. cit., p. 79.
64. B.J.C. Nos. 29–30; 19 July 1827; P.R.T. Gurdon, *The Khasis*, pp. 103–104; P.N. Dutta, op. cit., p. 80.
65. R.B. Pemberton, op. cit., p. 221; P.N. Dutta, op. cit., p. 80.
66. Home Public No. 30 C; 3 July 1863; J.C. Haughton to the Secretary Government of Bengal; J.N. Chowdhury, *The Khasi Canvas*, p. 287.
67. S.M. Ali, *The History of Jaintia*, p. 60.
68. P.N. Dutta, op. cit., p. 80.
69. S.M. Ali, op. cit., p. 60.
70. R.M. Lahiri, The Annexation of Assam, p. 174; H.H. Wilson, Document No. 12, Extract from a despatch from the Governor General in Council to the Select Committee of the Court of Directors, p. 16.
71. P.N. Dutta, op. cit., p. 81.

72. R.M. Lahiri, op. cit., p. 174.
73. Op. cit., p. 175.
74. P.N. Dutta, op. cit., p. 81.
75. Ibid.
76. R.M. Lahiri, op. cit., p. 175.
77. Ibid.
78. A.S.R. Letters received from Government, Vol. 1, 1834; Trevelyan to Robertson, 6 February No. 303; Rajendra Singh's petition to Governor General, 11 January 1834.
79. H.K. Barpujari, *Political History of Assam, Vol. I, 1826–1919*, p. 40; B.P.C. 1834, Nos. 141–143, February 6, Metcalf to Rajendra Sing.
80. H.K. Barpujari, op. cit., pp. 41–42.
81. B.P.C. No. 135; 10 April 1834, Jenkins 25 March.
82. R.M. Lahiri, *Annexation of Assam*, pp. 177–178.
83. P.N. Dutta, op. cit., p. 85.
84. B.P.C. No. 5, 23 February 1834, Jenkins to Macnagten, 13 January.
85. P.N. Dutta, op. cit., pp. 85–86.
86. R.M. Lahiri, op. cit., p. 185.
87. Home Public, No. 6–7A, 9 January, 1864; Letters of Lord William Bentinck Governor General of India to the Late Rajah Indro Sing of Jynteah.
88. R.M. Lahiri, op. cit., p. 185.
89. Home Public No. 30 C; 3 July 1863; J.C. Haughton to the Secretary Government of Bengal; S.M. Ali, op. cit., p. 60.
90. Home Public, op. cit.
91. Ibid.
92. S.M. Ali, op. cit., p. 61.
93. Home Public, No. 30 C; 3 July 1863, J.C. Haughton to the Secretary Government of Bengal
94. Ibid., S.M. Ali, op. cit., p. 61.
95. S.M. Ali, op. cit., p. 62.
96. H. Bareh, *The History and Culture of the Khasi People*, p. 158.
97. P.N. Dutta, op. cit., p. 87.
98. D.R. Syiemlieh, *British Administration in Meghalaya, Policy and Pattern*, p. 73.
99. Ibid.
100. Alexander Mackenzie, *The North-East Frontier of India*, p. 219.
101. D.R. Syiemlieh, op. cit., p. 73.
102. Ibid.

3

The Origins of the Resistance

The annexation and the disappearance of the *Syiemship* caused great shock and resentment in the hills. The plain tracts of the Jaintia Raj were incorporated into the neighbouring districts of Nowgong, Cachar and Sylhet. The plain tracts consisted of an area of about 3,850 sq. miles. Captain Fisher estimated that the Sylhet Plain tract alone in Jaintia would estimate about 650 sq. miles, the hilly tract an area of 2,340 sq. miles, the northern part 860 sq. miles.[1] A considerable trade in cotton, iron ore, wax, ivory, pan and cloth was carried out between the plains and the hills.[2] Jaintiapur for that matter was an important centre for all commercial transactions between the people of the hills and those of the plains. The annexation of the Jaintia Hills created a void in the life of the people. It would find expression first in their quiet acceptance of British rule followed later by their resistance to it.

First Administrative Measures

In order to understand the origins of the resistance, it will require a look into the period following the annexation of the Jaintia Kingdom and the developments that took place after 1835. It was held that "from the early part of 1835 till 1855, a period of twenty years, the people of Jynteah in the hills, appear to have been left almost entirely to themselves."[3] A policy of least interference was followed. The only alteration made in the position of the Jaintias appears to have been the relinquishment of the cultivation of the *Raj* lands, which were accordingly taken possession of by the *Dalois* of the villages.[4] However, there were some changes made in the tenure of office of the *Dalois* and their numbers. The number of *Dalois* was raised from twelve to fifteen. The *Dalois* were formerly appointed annually, but the Political Agent had extended the tenure of office to three years, the retention, however, depending on their good conduct. On the expiry of that period, the community had the right to re-elect another *Daloi*.[5] The government reserved to itself the paramount power, while the *Dalois*, on the other hand, were still retained as the head of the communes, with powers to dispose off minor cases.[6] No taxes were imposed on the people.[7] The Jaintias were allowed to continue their traditional practice of offering one he-goat from every village to the government as was the custom under the *Rajas*.[8] A report stated, "The people appear to have been very well contented with this state of things, which, however, was destined to have an end."[9] It appears that apart from the introduction of these administrative changes the people of the hills were left almost to themselves in their respective areas. Colonel Lister retired in 1854 and the charge of the hills was retransferred to the Commissioner of Assam, and Assistant Commissioner Hudson was deputed to discharge the duties entrusted to Colonel Lister and his assistant, Lieutenant Cave.[10]

As early as 1832–1833, Captain T. Fisher, Superintendent of Cachar, in his communication to Francis Jenkins had pointed out the mistake of David Scott of not realising any tribute from the Jaintia *Raja*. T.C. Robertson the successor of David Scott accepted the proposal and recommended to the government to include a new clause on the existing treaty with the *Raja* of Jaintia, providing for the payment of a tribute of Rs. 10,000 annually. The political agent being aware that a large amount of cash payment might be difficult for the *Raja* to realise, since all his subjects made their contribution in kind, the Political Agent proposed that a system of taxation should be introduced in his kingdom.[11] The Court of Directors thought otherwise and expressed their differences at the attempt, to force a tribute on the *Raja*.[12] In 1849, Colonel Lister suggested the imposition of a House Tax but the same was not approved.[13] In 1853, when A.J.M. Mills, an officiating Judge at the Sudder Court at Calcutta, who was on deputation in the North-East Frontier region of the then Bengal Presidency[14] visited Cherra, he was struck by the "proud and independent bearing" of the Jaintias and like Lister proposed a moderate house tax "to exact some payments however trifling the amount may be from the mountaineers of our possessions as a token of submission".[15] The proposal was however, turned down again by the Government of Bengal which meanwhile ordered an enquiry into the resources of the hills.[16]

1857 Uprising and N-E India

In 1855, the ex-*Raja* Rajendra Sing made an abortive attempt to retain the settlment of the former Jaintia kingdom.[17] This attempt was made in collaboration with the *Dalois* towards the restoration, gave added concern towards the problem. Meanwhile the outbreak of the uprising of 1857 in North India created much apprehension for the British. The soldiers of the 3rd Native Cavalry of the Bengal Army stationed at Meerut, a military cantonment some forty miles to the north of Delhi, rose in Mutiny against their British officers on 10th May 1857.[18] It subsequently spread to other parts of the country.[19] The revolt became general in Avadh, Rohilkhand and many parts of Central India. Delhi, Kanpur, Lucknow and Jhansi were the main storm centres,[20] there were other areas also that were affected. The southern part of the country was comparatively quiet though there were stray uprisings in places like Aurangabad and Kolhapur.[21] The Indian states but for some and the rest of the country side did not join the rebellion.[22] The event of 1857 was not to go without some repercussions in the North-East. Though the uprising might not have "produced the desired object of overthrowing British rule in Assam, but there is no doubt that the British power in North-East India was profoundly shaken in its very foundation."[23] British administrators did not agree with this view and they assert that the "great Sepoy Mutiny of 1857 left Assam almost untouched".[24] By the later part of July 1857, news of the revolt of Kunwar Singh in Bihar and of the Danapur regiment reached Assam.[25] A section of the Assamese aristocracy with the help of the 'Hindustani sepoys' stationed at Dibrugarh and Gauhati planned to overthrow British rule and install a descendant of the old Ahom ruling family, Kandarpeswar Singha, on the throne of Assam.[26] Meetings were held at Jorhat and it was arranged that the *sepoys* would rise simultaneously at different places, kill the Europeans and then march on to Jorhat to proclaim the descendant as the king of Assam.[27] The seriousness of the matter can be seen from the writings of the American Baptist Missionaries who had established themselves by 1851 in Sibsagar, Nowgong and Gauhati.[28] To deal with the critical situation, Major Hannay, Commandant of the regiment of Upper Assam, called in Captain Lowther, second in command, from Sadiya to the headquarters and concentrated the Gurkhas, Rabhas and Manipuris for any kind of eventuality.[29] The strategic posts in the border were closely guarded. B.W.D. Morton, Principal Assistant, Nowgong destroyed the bridges on the rivers Misa and Diju on the highway between Jorhat and Nowgong.[30] The differences among the leaders of the *sepoys* on the nature of attack and the time to revolt, gave ample opportunity for the authorities to take necessary steps. Major Hannay with the help of local informers secured the arrest of the officers and *sepoys* who were supposed to be implicated in the plot. He brought them to Dibrugarh where they were court martialed.[31] Captain Holroyd with a detachment of Gurkhas under Captain Lowther surrounded Kanderpeswar's residence at Jorhat on September 9 and arrested the Prince. Maniram Dutta, the *Dewan* and close associate of the Prince was arrested in Calcutta and was kept in the Alipore jail.[32] He was later sent to Assam where he was tried. He was convicted and hung.[33] Kanderpeswar, on the other hand, was first sent to Dacca and later was taken to Alipore jail. There were a host of others who were close to the Prince that were arrested. The arrest of the leaders of the revolt had broken the head of the conspiracy in Assam.[34]

Meanwhile on September 15, 1857, the ex-Jaintia *Raja*, Rajendra Sing offered to assist the Company to subdue the *sepoys* in revolt and with himself volunteering:[35]

> To proceed to Hindustan with my own troops about 2,500 Cookees, Khasis and Moneepuries to fight against the enemy of the British Government as I am bound to assist the

> Government agreeably to the Treaty No. 94 made on the 10th March, 1824 and should his Lordship be pleased to accept my service, then I beg an order be passed to furnish them with Muskets.

The ex-*Raja* also requested for an assignment connected with the management of troops destined to quell the prevailing uprising in the Upper provinces. The letter bore a seal, a circle four lines being inscribed in Bengali letters and a margin with the ex-*Raja's* signature.[36] The Government did not agree to the proposal and instead suspected the Raja for having some kind of involvement with the disgruntled *sepoys*. In a letter dated November 9, 1857, signed with a seal, the ex-*Raja* stated "that if his Lordship hold any suspicion on me on any occasion, therefore I beg his Lordship in Council where I dare say I could declare all the particulars and free myself from any charge."[37]

The Revolt of 1857 had also cast a deep impact in Cachar, at least for a few weeks.[38] This came about when three Companies of the 34th Native Infantry stationed in Chittagong mutinied against the Raj and having looted the treasury and breaking open the jail, they reached Cachar through Tripura and Sylhet.[39] Their intention was to join the disgruntled Manipuri princes and the Lushei chiefs who were at war with the British during this time.[40] Pitched battles were fought at Latu against Major Byang and his Sylhet Light Infantry. The areas that were affected by these operations were Binnacandy, Hailakandi, Sonai, Bhuban Lakhipur, Saraspur and others.[41] The British authorities were supported by the local *zamindars* and the tea planters in suppressing the cause of the *sepoys* who were at arms. After the death of Major Byang in the encounter at Latu, *Subehdar* Ayodhya Singh took charge and was successful in dispersing the *sepoys* who entered Cachar in several groups.[42]

Though the events of 1857 passed the North-East without any major impact, yet the aftermath and the reforms that were carried out in general had an important effect down to the Jaintias. The British had realized that "their bayonets were now the only real foundation of the Indian Empire and its preservation were dependent upon those military precautions which political security dictated in a conquered and an unfriendly land."[43] As far as military precautions were concerned care was taken to see that the number of Hindustani troops did not exceed their requirements where the events of 1857 would again be repeated. Towards this end, the Royal Army Commission went into the whole question of army reforms in India. Major General Sir Jonathan Peel who was the chairman of this Army Commission (which came to be known after him as the Peel Commission) submitted its report of March 1859 and recommended inter-alia[44] *i.e.*, an increase of the British troops and a corresponding reduction in the number of Indian troops. Care was also taken to see that the Indian troops should compose of different nationalities in order to avoid any kind of unification amongst them. The true intention of the British in creating dissention among the Indian troops can be seen from the writings of the Secretary of State, Charles Wood to the then Governor-General Lord Canning. In one of these letters dated 8th April, 1861, Wood wrote to Canning:[45]

> I never wish to see again a great army very much the same in its feelings and prejudices and connections, confident in its strength and so disposed to unite in rebellion together. If one regiment mutinees, I should like to have the next regiment so alien that it would be ready to fire into it.

The British had also realized that they could not do without the Indian Regiments. The importance of the locals in surviving the harsh climate of India and to undertake arduous military duties as seen in the Anglo-Burmese war of 1824 was clearly seen. The Peel Commission gave instruction that the hill tribes and the people of the frontier should be recruited into the army.[46] On the other hand, according to the provision of the Peel Commission, the 44th Native Infantry was reduced considerably[47] and what remained of that regiment was then scattered numbers of outlying detachments.[48] The reduction in the strength of the 44th Native Infantry was taken by the Jaintias as a sign of weakness on the part of the British,[49] for they did not know of the world outside their own and their knowledge of the power and resources of the Government was also most deficient. They were of the view that there were no more Europeans than the few they were able to see at Cherra, Gowhati, Sylhet, Cachar and Calcutta and that all the *sepoys* numbered no more than a few thousands whom they could easily drive away.[50] Meanwhile the suggestion of A.J.M. Mills of 1853, to impose taxes on the Jaintias was supported by the member of the Board of Revenue, W.J. Allen who was subsequently deputed to make a report by the Government of Bengal in 1858.[51] He revived the proposal of imposing a house tax, which he thought was to make the people realise the power of the British and make them "submissive to the authorities"[52] and to "acknowledge the supremacy of the government".[53] He further suggested an enquiry be made on the manner as to how the Raj lands were usurped by the *Dalois* and others.[54] In the changed situation, the Government accepted the recommendation of Allen and sent surveyors in 1859 to assess the collection of a house tax from the Jaintias.[55] In short the developments that were taking place in Jaintia Hills from 1835 and the failure of the attempt to restore the lost prestige of the *Raja* in 1855 down to the period when the surveyors were sent in 1859 to make assessment, had produced a good deal of excitement among the Jaintias.

Religion at Stake

Rev. T. Jones of the Welsh Calvinistic Methodist Mission at Cherrapunji when asked to write on the origins of the resistance noted that it: "cannot be attributed to any single cause".[56] The Jaintias had never been reconciled to the way in which their country was taken possession of by the British government. They were of the opinion that their *Raja* was sent to hold a friendly intercourse[57] with the officers, Captain Lister and Henry Inglis. The latter had been on friendly terms with the *Raja* and is said to have sent a message that he was coming on a friendly visit. According to the oral tradition, the Jaintias were of the opinion that, "Harry" (as he was called) Inglis was wanted by the British Political Agent on a charge of murder. Henry offered his service in subjugating Jaintia if he was absolved of the murder charge. If this oral tradition is correct, then it would appear that Inglis had taken advantage of his friendship with the *Raja* of Jaintia and had misled him about the true motive of the British. The *Raja* either believed in the friendly nature of the mission or thought it useless to offer opposition against the British did not resist and was captured.[58] The Jaintia look upon this act as a piece of treachery and a thing to be avenged whenever an opportunity offered itself.[59]

Apart from this tradition, the causes of the resistance can be understood from the other grievances of the people such as those indicated below. Following the recommendation of A.J.M. Mills, a police station was established at Jowai in 1855, as a token of the government's authority over the hills.[60] The location of the outpost in the heart of the village was resented by the people.[61] Once British administration was asserting its position in these hills, measures were taken to further control the Jaintias. One such step was taken by Rowlatt the Deputy Commissioner. He issued summary orders asking the people of Jowai not to burn their dead on the old site near the military outpost and that any infringement, thereof would be severely dealt with.[62] Each clan in Jowai had a separate cremation place and the one near the *Thanna* was that of the Dkhar clan. Later the Paswett clan was also stopped from cremating their dead within Jowai.The Langdoh and the Pakyntein clans were also stopped from burning their deads in those traditional burning places. Altogether seven or eight clans were suppressed from performing the last rites.[63] These acts on the part of the government official were looked at by the people as nothing but high handedness and affecting their religious beliefs. These places in fact were formerly outside the village but with the increase of population they fell inside it. It was asserted that "someone on enquiring by egg breaking (a custom which is still practised by the people to read out omens) process the cause, why one of his family was ill, learnt that it was because the old burning place of the tribe had been abandoned."[64] U Reang Dkhar of one of the affected clans gave a petition to the local government to restore back their traditional burning ground, but this request was turned down. The Jaintia found an unsympathetic government depriving them of ceremonies related to their dead.

To add to this concern, the people found that a large number of their women had been enticed to run away with the *sepoys*; they believed that this process would go on increasing so long as the *sepoys* would be allowed to remain so near to them.[65]

The establishment of a school by the missionaries also caused concern for the people. They were told that they must become Christians and to give up their time honoured *pujas* and that parents not sending their children to school and anyone worshipping or divining according to old usages would soon come to grief.[66] Though this was well intended, it was misunderstood by the people at large. The people were of the opinion that the missionaries were proselytising the masses by giving them free material assistance and thereby bringing them into their fold. They also stressed that since the majority of the people were illiterate, they were easily impressed by the material benefits given to them by the missionaries who were again backed by the government. The letters and despatches of David Scott and Francis Jenkins, Assam Commissioners from 1823–1831 and 1834–1861 respectively throws more light on the above assertion. It was found out that, the policy of the government was to bring over the missionaries and convert the people seeing that *Brahminism* had not made deep inroads and therefore there would be no repercussions from the plains.[67] In fact missionary activities in Jaintia Hills can be traced to the year 1842 with the arrival of Rev. Thomas Jones, who was accompanied by Lieutenants Lewin and Yule, to ascertain about the prospect of opening schools in Jaintia Hills.[68]

The Christian converts were trained in theology in those schools set up by the missionaries, and then sent to their own people for works under the church. The Welsh Presbyterian Mission would give stipends to students who were likely to return to their villages for church works or as school teachers. This, therefore, created a deep wedge among the people whereby those who lived in these special compounds considered themselves to be *"Skurs"* meaning school going and consequently more advanced and literate than those residing in the original areas which were known as *"Chnongs"*, in other words, meaning heathens.[69] Some Jaintias complained that their own people who were now converts had decried their own religion and taunted that they would have to give up their *Pujas*. No wonder when the Jaintias rose in resistance in 1860 and again in 1862 the Presbyterian Mission stationed at Jowai and the police station became their first target as they were symbols of the British Raj and therefore threats to Jaintia religion and their government.

The coming of the government officials and missionaries had other effects on the beliefs and practices of the people. The officials wanted the people to believe that the so called sanctity of their sacred groves known as *'khloo langdoh'* was a silly superstition of the unlettered people believing that gods or evil spirits dwell in them and that no harm would befell them if they disregarded such senseless sanctions.[70] The missionaries on the other hand played their own role in attacking the earlier practices of the people and their general attitude towards the hill tribes can be clearly seen from the remarks made by Rev. Jerman Jones. He said:[71]

> It was part of the standard of church membership that every candidate should not only have renounced all heathen practices but must also possess an intelligent knowledge of Christian principles.

Regarding the harvest festival he had this to say:[72]

> Harvest feast were not seemly for those who have learned to read the word of God. I was quite convinced that such feast were altogether unworthy of professed Christians and that an end must be put to them at once.

It is understandable, in the light of the above statement, that when Solomon Dohling, a police constable and one of the first convert from Cherrapunji, disregarding the belief and practices of the people shot a monkey in the sacred forest of Nangjngi located in the Jaintia Hills; he had to flee for his life.[73] In one of his letters to the Secretary, Government of Bengal, J.E. Haughton pointed out that "I have heard that U Choi Rungmot having some quarrel with Solomon about killing a monkey in the Dulloye jungle was the origin of the first rebellion".[74]

Taxes

The year 1860 was marked by the imposition of taxes and fresh revenues to be realised from the people which again was alien to their tradition. From the earliest times the Jaintias were accustomed to give just one he-goat to the *Raja* annually and to give voluntary service in the Raj lands whenever asked for. To their surprise, in 1860 the Jaintias were taxed. The house tax that was proposed by W.J. Allen, a member of the Board of Revenue of the Government of Bengal in 1858 was imposed on the inhabitants of Jaintia Hills in 1860 by an order dated the 28 March, 1859.[75] In the same year, judicial stamps was introduced and this was followed by taxation on fisheries which had hitherto been free from assessment. Further, in the same year, the people witnessed another imposition. The right to cut timber in certain forest areas was sold out to the highest bidder putting a stop thereby to the privilege of the villagers to cutting timber and collecting firewood and others which they had formerly enjoyed.[76] The amount that was collected from all these sources was minimal, but the introduction of these taxes coming in quick succession and at very short interval could not but produce inconvenience and resentment to people who had never been subjected to such taxation.[77] Moreover the people were loud in their complaints about the corruption and bribery prevalent at the Cherra court, and since they were strangers and did not know a word of the court language, they were ignorant of the law and were entirely dependent on, and at the mercy of, the native officials, who did not hesitate to grow rich at their expense.[78] The people used to say "we can do nothing, every case is lost whereas we give bribes".[79] In this regard the case of the Jowai *Daloi* may be mentioned: "U Den the Daloi of Jowai complained to Allen that in order to ensure his office he had to pay Rs. 350 to the mukhtiar of Inglis, son-in-law of the Political Agent, a gold mohur to Solomon, the interpreter and rupees fifteen to Rammohan, the treasurer".[80] Rev. Thomas Jones in his writings about the origin and causes of the Jaintia "Rebellion" states that "there is still a good deal of foundations for these complaints".[81] Rumours about increased taxation were many and "impositions of one sort or another were in fact appearing like mushrooms".[82] The people had heard about the Mutiny of 1857, and they were of the opinion that the new taxes were imposed as a result of the expense undergone in order to put it down. When they heard about the income tax, which was imposed in 1861, and the opium tax and others still under consideration, the people's mind were quite made up that the English were "determined to stay and fleece them".[83] It is in this background that the Jaintias caught the idea of gaining their independence and of freeing themselves once and forever from the hated 'Dkhar', as they call all foreigners. It appears that in this the people had the intention of driving away the British and restoring the *Raja*, though it is still not very clear whether the ex-*Raja* had a role to play in the outbreak of the resistance. Some assumptions were raised that "there seems some reasons to suspect that the villagers have been instigated to this rising by connections of the ex-Raja".[84] However, J.C. Haughton the officiating Governor General's Agent remarked in 1863: "I have never heard that anyone connected with the Jynteah Rajah instigated either the first or the second rebellion. I have never heard that anyone either from Sylhet or Assam instigated rebellion".[85]

Rowlatt's Unpopular Measures

Unpopular measures taken by the Deputy Commissioner Rowlatt aggravated the situation. Rowlatt had little time for the people to redress their grievances which they have been suffering for quite sometime. He was more busy with the supervision of the construction of the Shillong-Gauhati road. After the 1860, resistance to the collection of tax, Rowlatt took another step of disarming the people, a measure that was to stir unrest. He took away swords, shields and guns. These were the heirlooms which the people attached considerable importance to, as they needed them not only during their *pujas* but also for their own safety and protection, especially in a country infested with wild animals. To make matters worse, Rowlatt either sold or burnt their arms in their presence, thinking that these measures would prevent the people from resorting to arms. The official records estimated that somewhere around 588 shields, 457 swords, 14 guns and some spears were either confiscated or destroyed.[86] Meanwhile secret meetings were held in places such as Nongjngi, Shangpung, Nongbah and others. On 20 February, 1860, the Government *Tehsildar*, Solomon was prevented by the people of Nongjngi to enter the village and to enumerate their houses and collect the tax. It appeared that U Tma Pathor of Nongjngi headed the party of that village and refused to pay taxes. At Shangpung Giri Daloi held a meeting at the market place of Nongbah, where all those who were present objected to pay taxes to the British and it was resolved that if they had to do so, they would do it only to the Jaintia Raja. Furthermore, "on the 13th and 14th of the same month at the village of Mohfungkirting, close to the station of Cheerapoonjee"[87] a secret conference was held, which was attended by U Don Daloi of Jowai, Gopinath, the Bengali *Mukhtear* of the ex-Raja and around 400 other persons. U Yong Laloo of Jowai, a discharged agent of the Jaintia Raja gave a feast of pork. All those who had attended the meeting came to the same understanding as at Nongbah.[88] This was followed by open defiance of the government by the *Dalois*. They refused to obey the orders of the Government for the collection of the house tax.[89]

The Immediate Cause

The spark which caused the blaze was the incident that took place at Ialong. On the occasion of their traditional *puja* called "chad mastieh" a large number of people had collected to witness this traditional dance. Surki, a Khasi police officer of Jowai[90] on receipt of information that a large quantity of swords and spears had been collected on the occasion, went up and interrupted the *puja*, and seized all the weapons. It was alleged that, he forced the people to speak out, an act which was not permissible on such a solemn occasion.[91] Their former grievances of every kind were as heaps of gunpowder scattered in all directions and the Khasi police officer applied the torch to them, thereby setting the whole country ablaze.[92] Rev. Thomas Jones, the Christian Missionary has this to add in concern why the Jaintias took up arms:[93]

> As if this had not been enough, another of the Daroga pushed them on and forced them to run away into the jungles and by degrees to fight, that when the first insult was offered, they assembled in their durbars in order to consult as to the best way to have their grievances redressed, intending to settle everything peaceably, till this second Daroga told them that it was unlawful to do so, and that all who did come together into these Durbars and consult on anything of the kind would be taken up as Rebels and imprisoned and etc. It was after this they deserted their villages and commenced fighting .... It seems to me ... that they had made up their minds to fight immediately after the Jallong affair.

A local tradition has this to add, "the troops at Jowai used force and fired on the group of the local residents who came to deliver up their weapons".[94] This was corroborated by Rev. T. Jones when he stated that, the firing of the military guard on the people who came to give up their arms at Jowai as another cause of the outbreak.[95]

Going by the above discussion it is clear that the first phase of the resistance movement which broke out in 1860 cannot be attributed to a single factor, and that just like in the case of the second outbreak, a number of factors were responsible for the same. The annexation of the hills; establishment of a police station at Jowai in 1855; the activities of the missionaries from 1842, the destruction and desecration of the sacred groves and pools respective and a test of their religious sentiments caused alarm. Adding to the above, the limitation of the term of office of the *Dalois* and their judicial powers accompanied by the venality of the English courts and the attitude of the officials where people were oppressed created much misunderstanding and suspicion. The introduction of the house tax, judicial stamps, taxation on fisheries, aggravated the problem and served as the immediate cause of the first phase.

Before the commotion stirred by the introduction of the house tax had subsided completely, a new situation arose when the necessities of imperial finance imposed the income tax throughout British India.[96] The income tax came only a year after the house tax had been introduced. There were rumours of additional taxes on trade. The injudicious actions of some police officers in preventing the burning of the dead and the interference with the religious festival at Ialong and the firing of the troops on a group of local residents at Jowai gave rise to the immediate outbreak of the second phase of the resistance movement. The Jaintias rose in arms to protect their religion, retain their traditional administration and resist an alien rule.

REFERENCES

1. R.B. Pemberton, *Report on the Eastern Frontier of British India*, p. 223; H. Bareh, *History and Culture of the Khasi People*, p. 159; Alexander Mackenzie, *The North-East Frontier of India*, p. 220.
2. R.B. Pemberton, op. cit., p. 224.
3. Home Public Proceedings, 9 January, 1864, Nos. 6–7(A), Haughton to the Secretary, Government of Bengal, 3 July, 1863.
4. W.F. Trotter, *Report on the Administration of Jowai*, p. 10.
5. A.J.M. Mills, *Report on the Khasi and Jaintia Hills 1853*, p. 7.
6. H. Bareh, op. cit., p. 159.
7. Home Public Proceedings, 9 January, 1864, Nos. 6–7(A), Haughton to the Secretary, Government of Bengal, 3 July, 1863.
8. P.N. Dutta, Impact of the West on the Khasis and Jaintias, p. 99.
9. Home Public Proceedings, 9 January, 1864, Nos. 6–7(A), Haughton to the Secretary, Government of Bengal, 3 July, 1863.
10. Ibid.
11. Bengal Political Consultations, 5 November, 1832; No. 56, T.C. Robertson, 27 October; 7 January; No. 82, Robertson, 14 December 1852; P.N. Dutta, op. cit., p. 81.
12. P.N. Dutta, op. cit., p. 82.
13. A.J.M. Mills, op. cit., p. 13; H. Bareh, op. cit., p. 160.
14. John Hughes Morris, *The History of the Welsh Calvinistic Methodists Foreign Mission*, p. 142.
15. W.F. Trotter, op. cit., p. 11; Shobhan N. Lamare, "British Military Operations in the Jaintia Uprising of 1860" in *North-East India History Association Proceedings*, (henceforth NEIHA), 17th Session, p. 234.
16. P.N. Dutta, op. cit., p. 88.
17. Ibid.; Shobhan N. Lamare, op. cit., p. 234.
18. Jim Masselos, *Indian Nationalism: An History*, p. 13.
19. J.B. Bhattacharjee, "Mutiny in Cachar: A Survey of the Local Sources" in *NEIHA*, 4th Session, p. 35.
20. S.N. Sen, *History of the Freedom Movement in India 1857–1947*, p. 35.
21. Ibid.
22. Ibid.
23. S.K. Barpujari, "Further Light on the Revolt of 1857 in Assam", in *NEIHA*, 2nd Session, p. 237.
24. Edward Gait, *History of Assam*, p. 236.

25. S.K. Barpujari, op. cit., p. 237.
26. Ibid.
27. H.K. Barpujari, *Assam in the Days of the Company*, pp. 169–70.
28. S.K. Barpujari, op. cit., p. 237.
29. C.E. Buckland, *Bengal Under the Lietutenant Governors*, p. 154.
30. H.K. Barpujari, op. cit., pp. 168–169.
31. Bengal Judicial Proceedings, 1857, October 22, No. 178.
32. S.K. Barpujari, op. cit., p. 242; C.E. Buckland, op. cit., pp. 153–154.
33. C.E. Buckland, op. cit., p. 154.
34. S.K. Barpujari, op. cit., p. 242.
35. Cited in H. Bareh, op. cit., p. 160.
36. H. Bareh, op. cit., p. 161.
37. Ibid.
38. J.B. Bhattacharjee, op. cit., p. 35.
39. Ibid.
40. Ibid.
41. Ibid.
42. Edward Gait, op. cit., 2nd Edition, Calcutta, 1925, pp. 378–379.
43. T. Metcalf, *The Aftermath of the Revolt in India 1857–1870*, p. 227; Shobhan N. Lamare, op. cit., p. 234.
44. Imdad Hussain, "Aftermath of Mutiny: Army Reforms and the North-East Frontier 1861–1866" in *NEIHA*, 9th Session, p. 181; Shobhan N. Lamare, op. cit., p. 234. Interview with O. Kyndiah, N. Sutnga, R. Nongtdu, H. Shylla and others.
45. H.K. Barpujari, *Problems of the Hill Tribes: The North-East Frontier*, Vol. 2, p. 121; S.K. Barpujari, op. cit., p. 244.
46. H.K. Barpujari, op. cit., p. 121.
47. H.K. Barpujari, op. cit., p. 77.
48. Selection of the Records, Government of Bengal, Richardson to Deputy Adjutant General, 21 January, 1862; H.K. Barpujari, op. cit., p. 77.
49. Shobhan N. Lamare, op. cit., p. 235.
50. Home Public Proceedings, 9 January, 1864, Nos. 6–7(A) No. 1. A few hints on the origin and causes of the Jynteah Rebellion, by Rev. T. Jones.
51. P.N. Dutta, op. cit., p. 88.
52. W.F. Trotter, op. cit., p. 11.
53. P.N. Dutta, op. cit., p. 88.
54. W.J. Allen, *Report on the Administration of the Cossyah and Jynteah Hill Territory*, pp. 71–73.
55. K. Cantlie, *Notes on Khasi Law*, p. 103.
56. Home Public Proceedings, 9 January, 1864, Nos. 6–7(A), No. 1. A few hints on the origin and causes of the Jynteah Rebellion, by Rev. T. Jones.
57. Ibid.
58. S.M. Ali, *History of Jaintia*, pp. 60–61.
59. Home Public Proceedings, 9 January, 1864, Nos. 6–7(A), No. 1. A few hints on the origin and causes of the Jynteah Rebellion, by Rev. T. Jones.

60. Ibid., Home Public Proceedings, Haughton to Secretary, Government of Bengal, No. 30 C, 3 July, 1863; P.N. Dutta, op. cit., p. 88; J.N. Choudhury, *The Khasi Canvas*, pp. 310–312.
61. H.K. Barpujari, *Problem of the Hill Tribes North-East Frontier*, p. 80.
62. J.H. Morris, op. cit., p. 156; H.K. Barpujari, op. cit., p. 80.
63. Home Public Proceedings, 9 January, 1864, Nos. 6–7(A), No. 1. A few hints on the origin and causes of the Jynteah Rebellion, by Rev. T. Jones.
64. Ibid.
65. Ibid., H.K. Barpujari, op. cit., p. 80.
66. H.K. Barpujari, op. cit., p. 80.
67. Shobhan N. Lamare, "The Cultural Transition of the Pnars", p. 116 (Unpublished M. Phil dissertation).
68. J.H. Morris, op. cit., p. 88; on the 25th November, 1813, Mr. And Mrs. Thomas Jones sailed on the ship "Jamaica" for Calcutta from Liverpool. They arrived on the 23 April 1841 and their stay was prolonged by few more weeks in Calcutta because of Mrs. Jones sickness. After her recovery the two started on their lonesome and difficult journey, in small river boats, to the Khasi Hills. They arrived at Cherrapunji on 22nd June, 1841.
69. Shobhan N. Lamare, "The Cultural Transition of the Pnars", p. 123 (Unpublished M. Phil Dissertation).
70. R.T. Rymbai, "Christian Missions and the Indigenous Religion of the Khasi-Pnar" in Soumen Sen (ed.) *Religion in North-East India*, p. 85.
71. Ibid., p. 87.
72. Ibid.
73. Ibid.
74. Home Public Proceedings, 9 January 1864, Nos. 6–7 (A), Haughton to Secretary, Government of Bengal; Examination of a number of people, place and year, p. 19.
75. Home Public Proceedings, 19 May 1860, No. 39–40 (A), A.R. Young, Secretary to the Government of Bengal to the Secretary, Government of India, Home Department, 9 April, 1860.
76. *Selection of the Records, Government of Bengal*, Haughton to Eden, 3 July, 1863.
77. H.K. Barpujari, *Problem of the Hill Tribes North-East Frontier*, p. 78.
78. Home Public Proceedings, 19 May, 1860, Nos. 39–40(A), A.R. Young, Secretary to the Government of Bengal to the Secretary, Government of India, Home Department, 9th April, 1860; also Home Public Proceedings, 9 January, 1864(A), Nos. 6–7, Reports of Rev. T. Jones.
79. Home Public Proceedings, 9 January, 1864 (A), Nos. 6–7, Reports of Rev. T. Jones.
80. H.K. Barpujari, *Problem of the Hill Tribes North-East Frontier*, p. 78.
81. Home Public Proceedings, 9 January, 1864 (A), Nos. 6–7, Reports of Rev. T. Jones.
82. H.K. Barpujari, op. cit., p. 78.
83. H.K. Barpujari (ed.), *Political History of Assam*, p. 83.
84. Home Public Proceedings, 19 May, 1860, No. 39–40 (A), A.R. Young, Secretary to the Government of Bengal to the Secretary, Government of India, Fort William, 9 April, 1860.

85. Home Public Proceedings, January, 1864 (A), Nos. 6–7, Examination of a number of people, place and year, 20 April, 1863.
86. *Selection of records Government of Bengal,* Haughton to the Secretary Government of Bengal, 3 July, 1863.
87. Home Public Proceedings, 14 May, 1860, No. 134; Rowlatt to Jenkins.
88. Ibid.
89. P.N. Dutta, op. cit., pp. 88–89.
90. Ibid., p. 90.
91. H.K. Barpujari, *Problem of the Hill Tribes North-East Frontier,* p. 80.
92. Home Public Proceedings, 9 January, 1864 (A), No. 6–7, Reports of Rev. T. Jones.
93. Ibid.
94. H. Bareh, op. cit., p. 167.
95. Home Public Proceedings, 9 January, 1864(A), No. 6–7, Reports of Rev. T. Jones.
96. J.N. Choudhury, *Khasi Canvas,* p. 311.

4

The Course and Military Campaigns

In order to have a better understanding of the course of "the little war"[1] as it was called by an English language newspaper in India, the events may be divided into two phases. The events that had taken place in the year 1860 may be referred to as the first expression and those that took place between 1862 down to the last part of 1863 can be treated under the second expression of the Jaintia resistance movement.

The First Expression of Resistance

The relationship between the Jaintias and the British authorities, as seen from the previous discussion had become strained. At the same time it was noticed that though differences with the activities of the British officials had come about, the Jaintias did not take any step to challenge these new ideas which the foreigner government had introduced. The passive resistance that the people were carrying took a different turn altogether in the month of February, 1860. That month witnessed the submission of a joint petition given by the people of Jowai, Nangjngi, Changpung and Sutnga, requesting the government that they might be allowed to pay the taxes that was imposed on them, not to anyone else but to the Jaintia *Raja*. This petition of the people was refused on the ground that "no order existed for allowing such a request"[2] for the government *Tehsildar* had been appointed and the realisation of tax should be given to him. Meanwhile, Gopinath, the *Raja's* agent also sent a petition on the 13 February, the same year, requesting the settlement of the Jaintia Hill territory and at the same time stating that the *Raja's* pension of Rs. 500 a year was not sufficient for his client's support and that fresh arrangements should be made. A copy of this petition was forwarded to the Commissioner of Assam on the 14th of the same month.[3]

On 19 March, J.B. Shadwell, then in charge of these hills,[4] reported to Francis Jenkins Agent to the Governor General North-East Frontier that all the *Dalois* had agreed for the payment of the taxes.[5] There appears to be some problem with this assertion because on 21 March, the Magistrate of Sylhet informed Francis Jenkins, that the ex-*Raja* of Jaintia had arrived from Jaintiapur and stated that his people intended to rebel against the payment of the house-tax. Furthermore, the *Raja* informed that the people wished to make him their leader.[6] The British authorities reacted quickly and being apprehensive that the guard at Jowai, which was established in 1855 might be attacked,[7] a reinforcement of one *Havildar* and sixteen *sepoys* was sent from Sylhet on 22 March.[8] By this time news of the intended rising was pouring in from different quarters. Shadwell accompanied by Lietutenant Buist and 163 men of the Sylhet Light Infantry left Cherra on the 23 March. They were met by the *Havildar* and his men who informed them that they had been attacked by a large number of men and were forced to retire to the outskirt of Jowai with the loss of part of their baggage. This attack on the British camp at Jowai on 22 March, signalled the outbreak of the first phase of the resistance against the British.[9] By 28 March, more reinforcement came from Sylhet when Lieutenant Waterfield brought up one hundred men with him. Captain Scott by this time had moved towards Jaintiapur to occupy that place and also to join Lt. Buist and Shadwell at Jowai.[10] Meanwhile intimation of the rising was conveyed to A.R. Young, the Secretary to the Government of Bengal by the Commissioner of Dacca by telegraph. The Military Department of the Government of India was addressed with a view to the speedy issue of orders to the officer commanding the East India Regiment to take that Regiment on towards Sylhet and to the officers commanding at Dacca and to station there until further orders.[11] By 25 March, the fight had broken into full scale resistance. The Sylhet Light Infantry under the command of Lt. Buist was attacked and in the process a large number of the Jaintias were either killed or wounded. Shadwell on his arrival at Jowai summoned all the *Dalois* of the Jaintia villages and sent representatives to persuade the people to submit quietly and to pay the imposition. It was only after a few days that the *Dalois* from Mynso, Rymbai, Shangpung, Nongbah met Shadwell. Shadwell, however, suspected that the *Dalois* of these places were involved in the outbreak and therefore placed them under restraint and subsequently sent them to Cherra, where they were placed under confinement,[12] although, this was not the purpose for which the *Dalois* had come to meet Shadwell. This action augmented the tension that was already brewing. The Jaintias after suffering defeat at the initial stage, re-grouped themselves together and resorted in cutting off supplies that was meant for the British troops. Jenkins took measures to see that the resistance did not spread to other areas. Lt. Singer and Captain. Campbell were pressed into action. Major Richardson on the other hand was unavailable because of severe illness.[13] A proposal was also made at this stage by Jenkins to Lushington to have Captain Rowlatt in the Khasi and Jaintia Hills as a civil commissioner.

The pressure tactics that was used by Shadwell in imprisoning the *Dalois* worked out in favour of the British authorities. On the day after the *Dalois* were placed under restraint, the first sum of Rs. 300 was paid in on account of Giri Daloi of Shangpung. The tax was brought by the villagers.[14]

After having faced initial reversal, the Jaintias decided to attack Sylhet and to carry off the *Raja*. With this object in view they advanced to the plains during the night of 28 March, 1860. However, due to stormy weather that night, they were not able to reach Sylhet and being afraid to come during the day-time, they abandoned their intentions and proceeded towards Jaintiapur. On the way they plundered and burned the houses and made prisoners some of the *Burkandazes*. These groups were challenged by Lt. Ross, but before they could be arrested they had made good their escape to the hills.[15] On the same day, Lt. Buist and Lt. Waterfield, accompanied by Shadwell and along with a detachment of 1 *Subehdar*, 2 *Jamadars*, 8 *Havildars*, 8 *Naicks*, 4 *Buglars* and 188 *Sepoys* proceeded to visit some of the villages, especially those who had shown their displeasure.[16] They went first to Nongbah which by this time was almost deserted. Getting together a few of the villagers, they were asked to submit quietly and to give up the leaders in order to avoid molestation by the government troops.[17] The party then proceeded towards Nongjngi and it was here that Shadwell observes that there were a large body of men descending down the mountains and on which the village stands. The jungles at the foot of the hills were swarming with armed men and before the troops could do anything, the advanced guard of Lt. Buist was attacked. In the course of the fight a number of the 'rebels' who were trying to protect their stockade were killed. After suffering reversal, many of the Jaintias retired to the jungles, where they could not be followed.[18] The stockades that were erected by the people at the foot of the hills were destroyed. The troops started to pour into the village and destroyed some of the houses which were deserted by the people seeing the British forces advance.[19] This act of destroying the village was defended by Rowlatt. He wrote:[20]

> A portion of the rope of the tent which had been carried off from the guard that went out on the 22nd ultimo, to strengthen the post at Jowai and of which mention was made in a former report, thus clearly establishing that the people of this village was concerned in the attack of the guard, and as this was also the village from which the Tehsildar was first driven away, and as U Song Kuwar, the son of the ex-Rajah of Jynteah resided here, I have every reason to believe that the people were very inimical to us, and the principal actors in the rebellion and I therefore deemed it proper to punish them severely.

From Nongjngi the troops went to Nartiang, where they did not face any resistance. The leading people of the village presented themselves and agreed to pay the tax. The *Dalois* in the meantime had fled from the scene and Shadwell appointed U Sing as the new *Daloi* for life. The new *Daloi* and his men agreed to hand over those who had fought against the British.[21] Shadwell returned back to Mairang on the 31 of March, taking with him the five *Dalois* who were put under confinement. Jowai, on the other hand, was left to the charge of Rowlatt who was again accompanied by Captain Scott, second in command of the Sylhet Light Infantry with a *Havildar* party. They started from Mairang on the 12 April, 1860 and reached Jowai two days later taking with them the five *Dalois* who were taken by Shadwell.

In the meantime Lt. Ross with a party of the Sylhet Light Infantry who were instrumental in driving back the Jaintias who tried to sneak into Sylhet to kidnap the *Raja*, arrived at Shangpung. He reached Jowai on the 17th and reported that the country that he had passed through was quiet and that the people were giving up their arms.[22] Since the condition of the country on the whole was peaceful Lt. Ross returned back to the plains on the 18th of April, 1860. One of the principle leaders of the movement U Bakhir Pator of Ralliang surrendered to Captain Rowlatt on the 19th April, 1860. By the 22nd of April, most of the leaders had either surrendered or were captured. As the entire region was settling down, in consultation with Captain Scott, the authorities decided to send back all the men of the Sylhet Light Infantry to Cherra, except for a strength of 60 men to guard the stockade at Jowai and 50 to accompany Rowlatt on a tour to visit those villages which has not been visited by Ross. The party that returned to Cherra took along with them 12 prisoners and the revenue and arms that was collected and seized.[23]

While the detachment left for Cherra, Rowlatt and his men left for Shangpung on the 24 April, 1860 and reached there in the afternoon around 2.30 p.m. The people were coerced but refused to give their arms. In the process four of their leaders were arrested and taken to Ralliang where they reached some hours later. It was only when the people of Ralliang and Shangpung gave up their arms that the four hostages were released and some revenues collected.[24] The exact amount of revenue that was collected was not known as it did not receive any mention in the correspondence that was carried out by Rowlatt to Jenkins. On the 25th, Rowlatt and his men marched towards Mynso and by evening the people of this village and that of the neighbouring one, Shilliang Myntang gave up their arms. Next day the British troops marched for Nartiang through Nongbah. On the 27th, the troops halted at

Nartiang and all the villagers including "the notorious one Nungjoongee" (Nangjngi) delivered their arms.[25]

By this time most of the principal villages had been visited by the British troops and were disarmed and revenue was insisted for collection. The British troops under Rowlatt left Nartiang on the 28th, crossed the Umngot river which separates Jaintia from Khyriem Hima and returned to Cherrapunji on 1st May.

In their raids, shields, spears, swords were confiscated by Rowlatt and finding some of them "worthless and heavy articles to carry, I had them all burnt" he wrote.[26] A list of arms collected by Rowlatt has been given in Chart I below.[27]

Chart I

Name of Poonjee	Shield	Sword	Arrow	Guns	Spear	Powder	Pistol
Jowai	146	77	30	7	—	—	1
Ralliang	45	42	45	—	—	—	—
Shampoonj	77	63	—	2	3	2	—
Chilliang Monteng	35	31	—	1	—	—	—
Monsouh Poonjee	28	26	—	—	—	—	—
Nurteang	88	100	—	2	—	—	—
Nongjingnee	71	71	—	—	—	—	—
Nongbah	41	19	—	—	—	—	—
Sath Poonjee	47	46	—	1	—	—	—
Total	588	475	75	13	3	2	1
By Military Authorities	60	100	—	4	—	—	—
Grand Total	648	575	75	17	3	2	1

A number of prisoners were taken by Rowlatt to Cherra. They were either *Dalois* or *Pators* who were involved in the attacks on the British troops and the *thannahs* in the Sylhet district or men who had been actively engaged in carrying out the resistance.[28] The *Dalois* who were suspected to have been involved in the outbreak were dismissed from their offices and new ones were appointed in their places.

Aftermath of First Phase

By the month of May, 1860, peace was restored. After the suppression of the resistance the British decided to take under it the direct management of the Assam province and not to leave it entirely in the hands of the *Dalois*.[29] They felt that if this idea was abandoned then there will be little prospect of its improvement under the management of the *Raja*.[30]

It was further argued that since the *Raja* never resided in the hills and being a Hindu "he cannot be expected to have any sympathy with the hill tribes who have not adopted Hinduism as their religion."[31] Jenkins was also of the opinion that by handing the territory back to the *Raja* it would create problems for the development of its resources and at the same time retard the improvement of the neighbouring districts which were immediately under the British control.[32] The authorities were also of the view that if their supremacy was thoroughly established the revenue realised from the Company even in its present state would be sufficient to cover all the expenses of the necessary establishment to run the administration.[33] The demands, collections and balance of the revenue *i.e.*, the house tax during that period can be seen from Chart II.[34]

The first trial of strength between the Jaintias and the British ended by the month of May, 1860. The British had proved that a handful of disciplined soldiers could take charge of hundreds of undisciplined men. For the next one and a half years there was no sign of resentment but this was, however, a silence before another serious storm which would break out in the early part of 1862 and would drag on till 1863. This was to be the second phase of the resistance.

Interregnum

The events of 1860 ended like it had started, abruptly. Rowlatt was successful in quelling those who had revolted but what he failed to do was to understand the causes which had led to the outbreak. The British authorities, did not at all bother to look into the details and particularly into the aspirations of the people who held their freedom to be more important even in the face of increased British administration over their hills. Meanwhile, in 1861 news of fresh taxation was heard by the Jaintias even as the authorities were fully aware "that the imposition of new taxes would be sure to be attended with serious consequences" by the people unless the authorities

Chart II

Name of Elaka	Demand Rs. As P	Collections Rs. As P	Balance Rs. As P	Remarks
Nongfloot	268 0 0	268 0 0	— — —	—
Nurteang	1393 0 0	1363 0 0	30 0 0	Expected shortly
Muskoot	41 0 0	41 0 0	— 0 0	—
PunchPoonjee	400 0 0	168 0 0	232 0 0	Has been sent for
Shamphong	437 0 0	437 0 0	— — —	—
Darang	128 0 0	128 0 0	— — —	—
Nonba	390 0 0	390 0 0	— — —	—
Sootangah	493 0 0	493 0 0	— — —	—
Nurpo	210 0 0	190 0 0	20 0 0	Expected shortly
Munso	224 0 0	224 0 0	— — —	—
Amoie	188 0 0	188 0 0	— — —	—
Nongkhelleh	56 0 0	56 0 0	— — —	—
Sathpoonjee	715 0 0	683 0 0	32 0 0	Indispute
Sathpathor	243 0 0	243 0 0	— — —	—
Rumbai	671 0 0	434 0 0	237 0 0	Dolye gone to apprehend persons accused of plunder.
Chilling Monteng	353 0 0	351 0 0	2 0 0	Expected shortly.
Joowai	1082 0 0	960 0 0	122 0 0	Dolye ill expected shortly.
Ralliang	958 0 0	958 0 0	— — —	—
Nongjongee	520 0 0	520 0 0	— — —	—
Lakadong	333 0 0	145 0 0	188 0 0	Dolye lately appointed.
Rassee	28 0 0	28 0 0	— — —	—
Total	9131 0 0	8268 0 0	863 0 0	

take steps to counter challenge these oppositions.[35] The "state of public mind"[36] in the entire hill district about the imposition of taxes was also conveyed by Major E.H. Lushington, where the same was being conveyed by the latter to the Secretary, Government of India on the 3rd of January, 1862 and recommended the location of a small body of European troops in the hills.[37]

It would appear at this stage that there was much apprehension in the minds of the authorities as to what steps they should take as far as taxation was concerned and what would be the general attitude of the people towards the same, keeping in mind the events of 1860. This was the time when news about fresh taxes was rife and rumours were spreading fast. The *Darogah* of *thannah* Moolagool informed T. Smith the officiating Joint Magistrate of Sylhet that a *chowkidar* had given the information that the Jaintias were raiding the plains on the 15th or 16th of January. This was corroborated by a Brahmin returning from Jaintiapur who mentioned that "a descent was apprehended by the people of that place".[38] The ex-*Raja* who was made to retire and settle in Sylhet following the first phase of the resistance was contacted immediately and was warned that should any outbreak occur, he would in all probability be sent under arrest to Dacca or Calcutta, unless he could show evidence that he had worked on behalf of the Government by giving information or to take any such steps that was possible on his part as an ex-*Raja* to prevent such occurrence as the previous one.[39] Before all this there were already enough excitement in the hills. On 28 December, 1861, elaborate preparations were made for the annual dancing festival (*chad pastieh*) at Yalong, a place not far from Jowai. A police party from Jowai under U Solomon, a Khasi officer went to the dancing ground and prevented the people to continue with the dance. He then seized all the weapons that were used in this dance and dispersed the crowd.[40] The principal leaders, U Kiang Nangbah, U Kiang Pator, U Kma Langso, U Kiang Laso and U Chan Laloo protested against these acts and requested the *darogah* to give them three days time for the surrender of the arms as they were to celebrate the Myntang festival within that time.[41] But this was not accepted. Next day, a cremation procession was stopped at Jowai by the police as the administration had already prohibited the burning of dead bodies at the former cremation ground.[42] All these developments disturbed the Jaintias to a very great extent. The house tax of 1860, the income tax of 1861, news of fresh duties on trade and other commodities, the interference with the traditional festival at Yalong, the firing on the people of Jowai who came to deliver up their weapons and the activities of the missionaries went deep into their psyche. They were convinced that the alien rulers were determined to annihilate the indigenous culture and religion of the Jaintias. The resentment of the people was clearly seen when a *durbar* of the twelve *Dalois* was called on the banks of the *Syntu Ksiar* (golden flower) river to appraise the people about the intentions of the British. All these drove a deep wedge between the people and the British authorities.[43]

Oral tradition of the Jaintias refers to a resolution passed in this *durbar* that whosoever would dive into the bottom of the river and bring out a particular aquatic plant (*phlang Le tang*), would be recognized as the leader of the whole Jaintia people in their stand against British imperialism. In this competition Kiang Nangbah was one of the contestants. Many joined in the competition. U Kiang was successful. The *Daloi* of Nartiang garlanded Kiang with his armour and was chosen to lead the Jaintias in their fight against the British.[44] All these happened towards the close of 1861. Shortly after, a *durbar* was convened by Manik Daloi to urge the people to pay the tax but U Kiang Nangbah carried popular decision not to pay it. This was a clear defiance to the government's order to pay the tax. *Durbars* were hurriedly held in several places to plan the details of simultaneous action. The villages were barricaded, the stockades were raised at strategic spots and grains and other provisions stored in granaries. The old women and children were removed to dense jungles and caves, while the menfolk got themselves ready with arms to start the attack.[45]

Second Expression of Resistance

On the morning of 17 January, 1862, the villages of Jowai, Yalong, Latober, Shangpung under the leadership of U Kiang Nangbah and numbering around two hundred, stormed the police station at Jowai.[46] They also attacked the arsenal, burnt down the Christian settlement and besieged the military post.[47] The second phase of the resistance had begun. The seige of the military post at Jowai continued for a couple of days and *Jamedar* Khuruk Singh could only send a letter to Cherra through U Swet, a Khyrim cotton trader.[48] The messenger was held by the warriors many times but he managed to pass the letter to the Government authorities at Cherra. The passes from Jaintia to the neighbouring areas were closed and all the routes connecting the adjoining plain districts were guarded.[49] By 20 January, 1862, news of the Jaintias intending to attack the plain areas reached the British authorities. Steps were taken by the authorities at Sylhet where a company of the East India Regiment which comprised of thirty-five effective men and some fifty or sixty of the Sylhet Light Infantry were kept ready should the need arise.[50] This preparation caused much alarm in Sylhet and reports are there that shopkeepers hid their property and sending away their families.[51] The British authorities were in a disadvantageous position as the military base was considerably weakened by the reduction of the strength of the 44th Native Infantry according to the recommendation of the Peel Commission and the remainder of the regiment was a scattered number of outlying post in the north-eastern frontier region.[52] With the disappearance of the shopkeepers and the attempts that were made by the Jaintias in preventing the people from holding their usual weekly market, the military garrison was running short of food and other essential commodities.[53] In order to meet the shortage of essential commodities, Richardson in the morning of 21 January, sent from Cherrapunji thirty loads of provision escorted by a *Jamedar* and twenty-four muskets while a similar party was getting ready to move with essential commodities the following day to be accompanied by Richardson and Shadwell, the Political Officer incharge of the hills. Colonel Richardson and Major Rowlatt the Deputy Commissioner moved with a force of one *Jamedar* and 44 muskets to relieve Jowai where they arrived on 25 January.[54] The authorities in Calcutta directed the Commissioner of Dacca to send a detachment of the Eurasian Regiment stationed there by steamer to Sylhet, while from the Presidency the 28th and 33rd Native Regiments were sent. A full scale military operation was under way.

Military Campaign

This period witnessed the spread of the uprising to other parts of Jaintia Hills and the whole district for that matter presented a picture of an "uneasy state",[55] even an attack on the hill station of Cherrapunji was anticipated.[56] On 26 January, Lieutenant-Colonel Richardson and Major Rowlatt moved out to Yalong with a strength of 65 musket and a *Jamedar* to attack a stockade there. A serious fight broke out between the two opposite groups and in the process four *sepoys* were badly wounded. One of Major Rowlatt's police *sepoys* was badly wounded by musketry, one *coolie* was slightly wounded, one with an arrow as also were two or three *sepoys* and *coolies*, and many of the party were bruised by stones rolled down the hill.[57] The loss on the other side was not much, for the Jaintias made use of the dense jungle for their escape but the possibility of the wounded and the dead cannot be ruled out in such a fierce struggle. The stockade at Yalong was taken and destroyed and the party returned back to Jowai in the afternoon of the same day.

On the 27 January, Richardson commanding the 44th Native Infantry assisted by Major Rowlatt taking with them a party of one *Jamedar* and sixty-five muskets proceeded beyond Yalong to another place called Latoober to destroy a stockade that was built there. On reaching the place, the party found out that the stockade was well defended and in the rears and sides there were deep jungles and ravines. The route was full of hidden pitfalls filled with spikes. The route towards the stockade was shown by a native guide working for the government, but he could not make it far when he fell into one of the pitfalls and was severely wounded.[58] In this occasion the Jaintias attacked the party of Richardson with a dozen musket shots and then stones were thrown at them accompanied with showers of arrows. In this encounter the loss on the side of the government was the guide who was severely wounded and around twenty-five *sepoys* who were badly cut in their feet and legs with bamboo spikes called *'panjis'* hidden in the grass. The Jaintia loss was not much. Only one person was found killed inside the stockade and the majority of them had made good their escape into those dense jungles which surrounded the stockade. After capturing the stockade the soldiers resorted to burning of village. This was in line with the policy of Major Rowlatt in order to create a sense of fear in the minds of the people and to discourage them building stockades or fortifying their villages.[59]

Seeing the seriousness of the fights in the jungle terrain, Richardson requested the authorities to make arrangements for "Mountain Train guns" so that the menace could be tackled effectively.[60] The war was being carried out in dense jungle which enabled the Jaintias to attack the *sepoys* without being seen and in the process the loss on the part of the government *sepoys* kept on increasing. While the authorities in these regions were having their hands full with the trouble in Jaintia hills, another problem came up this time. It was reported that the Kukis were inclined to revolt on another frontier of Sylhet.[61]

On 5 February, 1862, a serious encounter took place in Shangpung. Lt. Col. Richardson assisted by 150 muskets stormed the village. A number of stockades were erected around this village. The lower stockades after it was stormed by two attacking parties was entered by three *sepoys* who were opposed by some villagers who managed to hide themselves till the storming party had passed. The *sepoys* were attacked with swords, on which they reacted and managed to bayonet their attackers. The fight was mainly carried out with muskets, arrows and stones and the steepness of the hills and the presence of the deep jungles and ravines worked in favour of the Jaintias. Nevertheless in this fight which was considered to be one of the most serious in the resistance, eleven Jaintias were killed including the leader U Giri Daloi.[62] Before leaving the village the army raided and burnt the houses. Most of the people who had resisted fled to Mynso a neighbouring village. The next day, the army visited Mynso and found a mound of wall erected for the defence of the village and was laid across the road. While the *sepoys* were climbing the rampant they were attacked by the Jaintias who were waiting for them. In the process one *sepoy* was severely wounded in the side by a musket shot. Moving further on, the advancing party came across two strong stockades and were attacked heavily. The stockades were, however, taken and the village was partially burnt. In this encounter one *Naick* was killed, one *Jamedar* and a *sepoy* were dangerously wounded, five others were wounded by musketry shots. On the side of the Jaintias two were found dead. One important reason as to why the fight in Mynso was not only difficult and different, was because the village was not only large but it was built on many separate hills and all were divided from one another by dense tract of jungles. These conditions necessitated the construction of many stockades and ramparts were erected and built. After dispersing the villagers the *sepoys* went burning on as much of the villages as they could find.[63] The wounded soldiers were sent to Jowai and fresh reinforcement were sought from Cherra and Sylhet. Major Rowlatt had also requested the 43rd Native Infantry stationed at Guwahati to move into Jaintia hills. The difficulty of the task in tackling the revolt can be clearly understood from the words of Richardson who wrote to a senior officer:[64]

> The tactics of the enemy are such as hitherto to baffle our attempts to punish them, and we have no object in again entering or occupying this village, which is far in the jungle, and where we could not keep open our communication without a considerable force. They have removed all their property and we have only burnt their empty houses. We can get but little information from the surrounding villagers, who stand too much in awe of the numerous bodies of the enemy scattered about in the jungles, and who, when attacked closely, at once leave their defences, and are lost among the rocks and jungles where we cannot follow them, for we don't even see them.

On 12 of February, 1862, fresh reinforcement from Cherra were received consisting of one *Havildar*, one *Naick* and sixteen *sepoys* with supplies. An army camp was established at Nongbah and army operations were mainly carried out from this camp. Leaving the camp under the charge of Lt. Udny who was again assisted by one *Jamedar*, two *Havildar*, six *Naicks*, one buglers and fifty-three *sepoys*. Richardson on 13 February, marched into the neighbouring village of Mynso with two *Jamedars*, six *Havildars*, eight *Naicks*, one buglers and eighty-three *sepoys*. At night the army camp was attacked by muskets which lasted for three hours but without not much of loss on the part of the British. The army collected as much rice as they could find which amounted to 200 maunds and after taking what they required was destroyed.[65] This was carried out intentionally to starve the villagers and those who had opposed the government, but the fight in Mynso was far from over. Richardson had another opportunity to attack Mynso again, but he could do this only if fresh reinforcement were made available. On 17 February, Lt. Buist joined the forces of Richardson at Nongbah with one *Subehdar,* one *Jamedar,* seven *Havildars,* six *Naicks,* two buglers and eighty-four *sepoys* and the plan to attack from three different areas in order to corner the leaders of the movement who had collected there. The plan that was formulated was executed on the 18 and 19 of that month. Three parties left Nongbah at three different times during the night and reached the village of Mynso before sunrise. A serious fight broke out. Lt. Buist with fifty men and a small howitzer attacked a large stockade and the people gallantly fought back killing a bugler and badly injuring a *sepoy*. He was soon assisted by Richardson but by this time the Jaintias of Mynso had already disappeared into those thick jungles which made penetration on the part of the British forces impossible. The stockade was ransacked by the joint force and the village burnt. Besides the above casualty, three others and a *Havildar* were badly wounded with arrows.[66]

On 21 February, Lts. Bartleman and Boyd of the 43rd Native Infantry from Guwahati arrived at Nartiang with eighty five men.[67] Meanwhile steps were taken along the border regions of Assam especially from Nowgong and Tezpur to check the intrusions of the Jaintias into that district. Capt. R.G. Chambers with a contingent of one *Havildar,* one *Naick* and eighteen *sepoys* marched over from Tezpur to assist the other detachments in that region.[68] In the plains of Jaintiapur, a *Jamedar* and forty three muskets were established to stand guard on the activities of the Jaintias, but Nowgong was not spared owing to its close proximity to the Jaintia Hills. On 25 February, a party of around 25 to 50 Jaintias attacked the Nowgong district and plundered the shops at a village named Ainsing and carried off the goods from other traders. In the process, one *Kyah* merchant named Sook Deo was killed.[69] Apparently this was carried out by the Jaintias in retaliation to the steps taken by the British authorities and the army in destroying their villages and their basic means of subsistence.

In the meantime, E.A. Rowlatt had returned to Jowai from Nongbah. Rowlatt proposed to Major Hopkinson, Agent to the Governor General North-East Frontier about the recruitment of Khasi *sepoys* in addition to the present force to be placed under the orders of the Jowai *darogah*. The Deputy Commissioner was of the opinion that "unless a body of this nature is raised I see no probability whatsoever of the rebels leaders being apprehended."[70]

Jaintia under Martial Law

The state of affairs in Jaintia hills was taken very seriously by the authorities in Bengal. Major Henry Hopkinson and Major Rowlatt had proposed that the country be proclaimed to be in rebellion and to place it under martial law. The officers were convinced that the disturbance was far from being suppressed and it was still the same as it was on the first day when the troops entered the fight. Though the troops had occupied the villages of Jowai, Nartiang, Amwi and others, yet the outbreak had spread throughout the length and breadth of the Jaintia country. Stockading were once again constructed all around the villages of Nartiang. In the south and west of Nartiang, Yooksi, Koodeng, Nongbarai villages were all stockaded. Furthermore, the mountain passes through Borkhat and Moorabee were closed by defences thrown across them for the purpose of preventing the entrance of troops through the hills by those routes. The main road into the hills from Jaintiapur was also closed. In order to tackle the situation Rowlatt further suggested that the provision of the Arms Act for the disarming of the people should be put in force and to be carried out with utmost rigour. Regarding trials, convictions and sentences he proposed that "it should be carried out on the spot by a military tribunal",[71] instead of being conducted by a sessions court.

As the resistance continued the British forces had to muster what for the Jaintias was a formidable army. On 7 March, 1862, Capt. Robinson of the 28th Regiment Punjab Infantry started from Jaintiapur and sent the regiment to the hills in two detachments. One group came by boat and since there was great scarcity of boats one group went up on elephants across the country. It only in the afternoon of the same day that they reached Nongtalang. On 9 March, Robinson along with one Captain, one Assistant Surgeon, one *Subehdar*, one *Havildar*, three *Naicks*, one bugler and thirty *sepoys* moved towards Sohkha to destroy the stockades that were built there. On reaching the stockade, Robinson was attacked on both sided by a "volley of arrows and stones".[72] The passes by which they had entered was occupied, and Robinson had to return back to Nongtalang by another road with the help of a local guide. In this fight six of the Jaintias were killed. On 12 March, Richardson along with Major Rowlatt and Lt. Buist with forty muskets moved from Padu towards Nongbarai to destroy its stockades. The road towards Nongbarai were again blocked by felling down trees and digging *panji* pits. Lt. Buist was assigned the task of destroying the stockades that were not defended. Richardson and Rowlatt, on the other hand, started to move into the village. They were resisted but it was not for long before the people were dispersed. The village was burnt and the stockade was destroyed. This consisted of a wall of stones about five feet high and five feet thick and extended all around the sides of the village. They also visited Koodeng where the inhabitants surrendered and from whom was collected six muskets, swords, bows, arrows and shields. The village was not burnt but the stockades were destroyed.[73] In retaliation and in order to keep the British forces from the hills the Jaintias resorted to raid the plain areas of Nowgong again. On 14 March, the Jaintias numbering around 150 in number went into Nowgong district. They retreated back along the lines of the Kupli river only after they were challenged by Mr. Ingels the Extra Assistant Commissioner. A number of arms were recovered from the retreat.[74]

By the middle of March, the attempts made by the British authorities to curb the outbreak were not successful and there were no "extraordinary success" on their part.[75] The authorities were, however, banking on something else. Hopkinson was of the opinion that the Jaintia's opposition would automatically collapse when food would begin to become scarce, and the season for cultivation arrives where the majority of the people would go back to the villages.[76] At the same time he was also aware of the fact that, were the troops to withdraw, it would encourage the people to rally again and challege the authorities.[77] Ironically the scarcity of food was to hit the British troops first. The troops stationed in these regions had to depend heavily on the supplies that were coming in from Cherrapunji. This was not enough adding to the trouble in clearing those passes that were constantly monitored by the Jaintias. With the lack of food, sickness was not unexpected until immediate supplies could be drawn from Dacca.[78]

While the authorities were busy making lists of small detachments to be placed in the hills and how to procure essential commodities North Cachar was attacked. This occurred on 17 March, 1862.[79] Sylhet was next attacked. About forty Jaintias armed with *daos*, arrows and muskets attacked Polasgooree, in Mouzah Nillee and plundered all the place. In the process two Lalung women were injured. This took place on the 23 March.[80] This was a deliberate attempt on the part of the Jaintias to keep the British authorities busy in the plains. On 20 March, Col. Dunsford and the other officers attacked Ralliang. Earlier Maj. Rowlatt had received intimation from his spies that Ralliang was strongly stockaded. Dunsford moved from Shangpung with two detachments, four European officers, six native officers, 198 rank and file belonging to the 28th Regiment Punjab Infantry and four European officers, three native officers and 174 rank and file belonging to the 44th Regiment Native Infantry.[81] This was a formidable force when compared to the Jaintia strategy of village defence.

These military developments indicate that the Jaintia resistance was far from over and that the British authorities were much concerned. Accordingly on 22 March, 1862, Brigadier General St. G.D. Showers, Commanding the Presidency Division issued a confidential circular to all the officers commanding the several detachments in Jaintia Hills for the suppression of the revolt. Some of its provisions were as follows:[82]

(a) All men found in arms must be treated with that severity which open hostility to the state demands, and the chiefs of these villages which are known to have been the principal instigators in the insurrection must have no terms granted to them. The government alone can deal with them. They must be confined and made over to the civil officer who may accompany the detachment.

(b) All stockades and fortified posts must be levelled with the ground; all villages in arms must be attacked, and, after they are taken, the villagers should have the option of returning to them.

(c) All Jaintias who come in must give up their arms, after which they will be allowed to enter their homes and etc.

It was in the background of the above developments that the authorities in Fort William took serious note on the proposal put forward earlier by Hopkinson and Rowlatt on 4 March, 1862 to declare that the whole of Jaintia Hills as being in rebellion and to place it under martial law. On 26 March, E.H. Lushington, Secretary to the Government of Bengal, in his letter to the Commissioner of Assam stated that "the sanction of the Government of India has this day been solicited to the issue of a proclamation, under Clause I, Section III of the Act XI of 1857 declaring the Jynteah Territory to be in a state of Rebellion,"[83] and commissioning Major Hopkinson, Major Rowlatt and Colonel Richardson to try all offences within their jurisdiction. On 28 March, 1862, Brigadier General G.D. Showers of the Eastern Command was placed by the Government of India in exclusive civil and military charge of the Jaintia Hills above the authority of the Commissioner of Assam.[84] By a proclamation under Act XI of 1857, G.D. Showers, Rowlatt and Richardson were empowered to try all offences referred to in that Act.[85]

On 27 March, Major Longmore and Lt. Walcott commanding the 33rd Native Infantry marched towards Sutnga and Bataw. In time apart from the regiment that was first in operation in these hills, there was also one battalion of the Eurasian Battery, four battalions of the 44th Native Infantry and one battalion of the Bengal Military Police. The troops wherever they went stormed the villages, burnt the houses and destroyed the stockades and granaries. Such retaliation on the part of the British authorities made the people more determined to resist the British. The recovery of guns and pistols from those killed or apprehended suggests that the people were able to procure firearms from the neighbouring areas. Encounters of the most serious nature were reported from Shangpung, Nartiang, Sutnga, Nongkhlieh, Rymbai, Bataw, Ralliang, Barato, Mookaiaw, Chilliang Myntang and others.[86] In this phase of the resistance a large number of people including innocent women and children lost their lives. At least on one occasion several women and children were drowned in a stream while trying to escape from the vengeance of an advancing military column.[87] The casualty on the British side was also very high. A number of the European officers commanding the troops either died or received serious injuries.[88] Patrolling were carried out in Mynso, Sutnga, Yalong, Bataw, Iooksi, Pompadong, Nongbarrai and Koodeng. Capt. Robinson who was patrolling the southern region reported having taken eleven firearms of sorts, twenty-six swords, twenty-seven shields, 108 bows and 260 arrows.[89] Concern was growing about the non-availability of food grains. It was also noticed that the people had not returned to their villages to prepare their fields for the seeds to be sown. Dunsford was of the opinion that "unless the fields are sown within the next ten days there will be little prospect of a crop," and the people are reported to be already suffering from dearth of food.[90]

The measure that were taken by the Deputy Commissioner and his colleagues did not go unmonitored by the authorities in Fort Williams. The latter were of the opinion that Major Rowlatt did not make an attempt to enquire into the causes of the insurrection but whereas his duty required him to make an attempt.[91] Meanwhile, G.D. Showers who had taken charge as the Commissioner of Khasi and Jaintia Hills arrived at Jowai on 13 April, 1862. The following day Showers issued a proclamation from his headquarters, Jowai. The proclamation stressed that the government had established with authority that Act XI of 1857 be brought into force in the Jaintia Hills. The people, it suggested, had continued head strong with the resistance, and now the severe laws that were established would take its own course. The Commissioner called on the people to assist him in restoring the peace of the district;[92] at the same time he warned the inhabitants of the district that all who were found harbouring the 'rebels' or supplying them with provisions, or in any way assisting them, would render themselves liable to the penalties of the Act. Showers exhorted the people to give up those who were threatening to the government. He pointed out that the British Government had no wish to inflict the miseries of a severe law on the people and urged them to apply for pardon so that their grievances could be redressed. He added that no complaints would be received as long as the people are in a state of insurrection.[93]

Meanwhile, Rowlatt who did not manage to find favour with the authorities of Bengal because of his activities and high handedness in handling the problem in the hills was replaced by B.W.D. Morton. Morton had made his mark as an administrator in successfully handling the Garo affairs.[94] Immediately after taking charge, Morton declared general amnesty to all[95] who had not been engaged in "cold blooded murder" with the exception of U Kiang Nangbah and U Mullon.[96] The term "cold blooded murder" did not include the deaths of *sepoys* killed in fair fights. In order to speed up the surrender of the Jaintias, Morton resorted to economic blockade in order to starve those who were at war. In this regard an intimation was made to the Commissioner of Assam to close the *hats* at Nowgong.[97] Lt. A. Andrew the Assistant Commissioner of Khasi and Jaintia Hills was also of the same opinion and pointed out that the people were obtaining more of their supplies from that quarter. He added further that the *bazars* on the side of the Jaintia Hills should be closed including the *hats* in the territory of the *Khyrim* Syiem and if this could be done the people would be checked from procuring articles of food and force them to surrender.[98] The other methods that which Lt. Andrew wanted to carry out was the burning of the villages[99] but this did not find its approval with Morton who otherwise suggested that the villages should place themselves and their property under the protection of the guards and to unroof their houses.[100] By doing this Morton hoped that the people who were in arms would be prevented from taking up their quarters in the village and at the same time not exposing the inhabitants to any great hardship. However, with regard to Chilliang Myntang, Morton has this to request "I beg you will request Lt. Campbell to destroy any houses which interferes with the safety of his position".[101]

The troops and the police adopted vigorous measures to suppress the insurgents and to stop mobilisation between the Jaintia camps.[102] The *hats* at the Nowgong frontier were now closed and troops were stationed there. A body of police was also placed at Puriang to prevent the Jaintias from getting supplies from the Khyriem state. In this context military operations were carried out but the troops suffered with adverse results in a fight near Mynso. The 33rd Native Infantry Regiment was attacked heavily and in the process 8 *sepoys* and 2 *coolies* were killed on the spot and some dangerously wounded. The Jaintias made good their escape with 7 muskets and ammunition taken from those who had been killed.[103] Another serious fight broke out when the troops laid siege of a Sutiang stockade at Nongkhlieh. The government regiment operated from a valley against the stockade on the opposite Sutiang ravines where the Jaintia warriors were lodged. The Jaintia camp was composed of volunteers from Shangpung, Rymbai, Nongkhlieh, Sutnga and the neighbouring *Daloiship*. The Jaintias withheld the siege for more than six months. Soldiers were mobilised to continue the operations. A large number of soldiers were killed in the fight. The soldiers could not trace from where the arrows came. It was only with the help of one cloth merchant from Rymbai who pointed out their hideout on being paid a large amount of money that the soldiers reached the stockade and traced the arrows to a canebrake. U Ksan *Daloi* of Nongkhlieh escaped.[104] Those persons who were working as informers to the government were paid good sum of money is well established. The British would use informers for the capture of the principal leaders, as shall be indicated presently.

Lull During the Campaign

The period between April and August 1862 did not see any fierce encounter except for some seiges of some villages. Though few encounters took place during this time the British military operations were never entirely suspended. In most cases the troops acted on the defensive. The reasons for this were; the inconvenience of moving troops from one quarter to another during the rainy seasons; the unhealthiness of the 33rd Native Infantry; the absence of a considerable portion of the 44th Native Infantry; and it was decided that no active movement should be carried out while negotiations with those in arms were going on lest it would serve to arise the suspicion of the people about the sincerity of the government in carrying out the same.[105]

By the middle of August steps were taken to countercheck the activities of the Jaintias. The earlier methods of carrying out economic blockade had not succeeded because the attempts to starve those at arms had resulted in positive injury to the larger section of the people, and even those who were loyal to the authorities started to doubt the true intention of the British. To this effect Major J.C. Haughton, Agent to the Governor-General, North east Frontier, had earlier cautioned the Deputy Commissioner Captain B.W.D. Morton to "abstain from all initiatory action whatsoever"[106] and not to "close markets nor destroy houses or villages while continuing the policy of conciliatory."[107] Meanwhile the authorities were trying to understand the root cause of the problem and as to why the Jaintias were so adamant in carrying out the struggle. The earlier reports which Rowlatt had submitted were not impressive to the authorities. Even the reports of Morton did not find strong favour with Major J.C. Haughton, when he stated that "the rebels had no substantial grievances".[108] Haughton was of the opinion that the people "had several, but you yourself mention one which, even in civilized countries, would be likely to lead to violent disturbances." He further added "I allude to the arbitrary suppression of their religious observances."[109]

> I would also wish to know what has been done to the person or persons who were guilty of this outrage. Had the government been fully informed upon the subject, I do not think that any authority would have been given for the introduction of either income or license tax among a people so little able to understand such measures .... I beg to be informed whether any representation was made upon the subject.

Still more Haughton has this to inform his subordinate:[110]

> You appear to labour under a mistake as to the policy of the government towards these hill tribes. It is the wish of the government to leave to them as much as possible the management of their own affairs.... It was the destruction of weapons (much esteemed, apparently as heirlooms) which was one great cause of the rebellion. I would, therefore, request you not to insist on surrender of weapons at any rate.... In most jungly countries weapons are necessary to the preservation of life from wild animals and a rule which might be just and proper in the plains of Bengal, in Oudh or the Punjab might act most oppressing in such a country.

When the rainy season had ceased and anticipating the movements of troops, the Jaintias resorted to interfere with the couriers of information so that military operations would be obstructed or at best delayed. To this effect, they started attacking the *dak* carriers and in one such case on the 28 August, 1862 the *dak* carriers who were *sepoys* carrying arms belonging to the 33rd Native Infantry moving from Nartiang to Chilliang Myntang were attacked. Morton assigned "the loss of so many men to the cowardice of the non-commissioned officer in command."[111] It appears that a number of *sepoys* had perished but the authorities remained silent about the actual number of persons killed.

The "Little War"[112] which the British were fighting in these parts of the hills dragged for longer than what they had anticipated. The war had assumed larger proportions and had become expensive.[113] The Jaintias were quick to rally when ejected from one stockade and the type of jungle warfare that they were carrying out, "as this is just what they excel in"[114] could easily "tire out any regular troops".[115] To a request made to the Military Department in Bengal, to send more European officers, by 30 August, four European officers of experience were sent to carry out military operations with the 44th Native Infantry Regiment. A note of caution was also added, where the authorities in the hills should refrain altogether from burning of villages and otherwise indiscriminately harrasing the people.[116] The activities of the police station which were regarded as "necessary evils"[117] in different parts of the region were looked into. The army officials had realised that without the assistance of the police officials it was difficult for them to get information but at the same time it was felt that "it is of the greatest importance to keep a careful watch over the proceedings of the police themselves."[118]

By September, it was feared by the British that the destruction of the people's granaries and the suspension of agricultural operations throughout the greater part of the disturbed country which had already produced great distress and since cultivation was not carried out, it was likely that the scarcity would be felt more severely before the next harvest. It was believed that the people had neither food to eat nor the means of buying it.[119] At the same time there was another apprehension, that perhaps, that the people had suspended the fight for sometime in order to procure and store food crops and once this was met they would renew their resistance.[120] In order to check this move the British authorities made use of the Khasi chiefs to mediate with the Jaintias and especially with U Kiang Nangbah who by this time was the de-facto leader of the Jaintia resistance. In this context, Raja Rabon Sing of Khyriem and Raja Ram Sing of Cherra were deputed as emissaries of the Government to initiate negotiations with the 'rebel' leaders.[121] U Kiang Nangbah and his followers, however, raised clear demands that the people should be exempted from any kind of taxation, that there should be no interference with their traditional religious rites and that their *Raja* should be reinstated and that troops and the police should be withdrawn from the Jaintia Hills.[122] Meanwhile on 3 October, 1862, thousands of Jaintias had assembled at Shangpung to speak with the *Kunwars* (the family members of the ex-*Raja*) and to see the gold sword, the property of the late *Raja* of Jaintiapur.[123] Even the *Kunwars* were used by the British authorities to mediate on their behalf. The mediators were not able to convince U Kiang Nangbah and his followers. U Kiang moved from place to place in the hills to keep up the morale of the people and to inspire them to evade payments of any kind and to perform all customary rituals. On the other hand, some Jaintias were instrumental in providing information to the British. In this sense a reference can be made of one Hajin Manik of Shangpung who gave information to the British authorities about the plans and intentions of the people and how U Kiang Nangbah tried making contacts and sought help from the Burmese King[124] and the king of Russia.[125] It may be mentioned here that the earlier reports on the course of events of 1862 does not give any references of such outside contacts.

Resort to Arms

The failure of negotiations emboldened the authorities to resort to vigorous military action. The members of the erstwhile ruling family at Jaintiapur were kept under surveillance. Steps were also taken by the authorities to recruit Khasis and to act in concert with their troops to which the *Syiem* of Cherra Ram Sing and that of Khyriem, Rabon Sing had agreed.[126] They were also convinced that the people of Jowai under the leadership of U Kiang Nangbah was spearheading the movement and the success against the people of Jowai would result in the submission of the entire country.[127] In this regard the 21st Native Infantry Regiment was asked to move to Jaintia Hills to assist the 33rd Native Infantry which was not doing well on account of sickness of the *sepoys*. Adding to this a number of detachments with considerable strength was placed in vulnerable areas of Jowai, Nartiang, Mynso, Nongbah, Chilliang Myntang, Sutnga, Borkhat, Bataw, Nongtalang, to check the movements and operations of the Jaintias. Furthermore, "two columns of at least 100 strong each, accompanied by 50 friendly armed Khassyahs, to be employed in dispersing armed bodies of rebels. The Sylhet frontier to be guraded by the Furreedpore Regiment. That of Assam to be similarly guarded by the local corps and wing of Sikhs. A detachment of the local corps (43rd Native Infantry) 100 strong, to be provisioned from Assam, be pushed up under the command of an English Officer beyond the Mikir frontier in the direction of the Nongfloot Illakah, to patrol that part of the country and give the Mikirs confidence."[128] In all there were around 5000 to 6000 troops and police operating in the hills during the later part of this phase of the resistance.[129]

In the beginning of November, renewed offences were carried out by the troops. In order to confuse the military operations the Jaintias again threatened Cachar and Cherrapunji. A large number of Jaintias were reported to have gone eastward towards North Cachar.[130] Cherrapunji during this time was in a state of alarm. On 8 November, an attack was made on the village of Terriaghat[131] ten miles from Cherrapunji.[132] The Jaintias surprised and burned the place, killing some of the inhabitants, several police and two or three Bengali traders (called box wallahs) who were on their way up to Cherra to sell their wares. It was feared that the Jaintias would come up the hill and attack the station during the night, and had they done so they might have easily plundered and burned the houses and killed many of the residents for the scanty garrison of *sepoys* and police which was quite insufficient for the protection of the whole station.[133] On 7 and 8 November, telegrams were sent by Morton to the authorities in Calcutta requesting for assistance from the Kamrup and the Punjab Regiments along with mortars as the 33rd Native Regiment was made ineffective due to sickness. Bholagunge a village on the road to Sylhet was also attacked by the Jaintias. Seeing the seriousness of the turn of events, strategies were worked out as to how the menace could be curtailed. The 28th Native Infantry that was stationed at Guwahati was asked to move to the hills from the north. The detachments of the 44th Native Infantry in Cachar and Sylhet was called in, and the Eurasian Artillery at Dacca was sent to Cherrapunji with mortars. Colonel Dunsford who was commanding the 28th Native Infantry was placed to direct military operations of the whole force. The first battalion of Bengal Military Police was sent to Cherrapunji. Besides these, the Sikh and Gurkha Regiment was also brought in. The Sylhet and Cachar frontier was guarded by the 33rd Native Infantry and the Kamrup Regiment. The northern part of the Assam frontier was guarded by the 43rd Native Infantry with its headquarters at Guwahati. It was also intended to arm a company of Native Infantry Regiment of the force with two-grooved rifles. *Coolies* were also raised and brought in from as far as Chotanagpur to carry baggage and supplies for the troops. Ponies were also used for the same purpose.[134] Fort William authorities also approved the request made by Brigadier General Showers that the Eurasian Artillery should be accompanied by two 5½ inch mortars to be sent from Fort Williams with a suitable supply of ammunition and be moved to Cherrapunji should their service be required in this operation.

To add to the increase military presence, administrative measures were also taken. The proclamation under Act XI of 1857 issued on 2 April was revoked on the 18 of November, 1862.[135] The Commission to try offenders was re-introduced, and a reward of one thousand rupees was offered for the apprehension of U Kiang Nangbah and a reward of five hundred rupees for each of the other *Dalois* and leaders whose capture was likely to hasten the pacification of the hills.[136] Meanwhile the *Kunwars*[137] were asked to return to Sylhet as "their presence in the hills tends to excite the rebels".[138] On 26 November, the Kamrup Regiment under the command of Lt. F. Henderson was attacked near Terriaghat by a strength of 500 Jaintias.[139] By 1 December, the plan of operation to be pursued against the Jaintias was carried out. Captain E.K.O. Gilbert, Assistant Adjutant General of the army, Presidency Division noted: that the first objective was to secure the base of operations and for this purpose two companies of the Kamrup Regiment should be posted at Sylhet and Cachar under a European Officer. Secondly, the Collector of the district should keep a strict watch on the parties coming down to the plains either to plunder or to carry out supplies and to give immediate intelligence to the officer in military command. Thirdly, a regiment of not less than 180 rank and file should always be present at the headquarters. Fourthly, troops should be stationed at Nongkhlaw, Mawphlang, Shillong, Puriang, Nongkrem, Moosynting in order to check the movements of the Jaintias. Fifthly, two regiments should be stationed at Jowai. This would allow the outpost to be relieved periodically, and would also enable the officer commanding the district to move out at any moment with a sufficient force to any part of the District.[140]

Detachments were also sent to outlaying Amwi, Nongbah, Mynso, Yalong, Latoober, Shangpung, Nartiang, Jaintiapur. The Third Regiment was divided into two wings. The headquarters and right wing was stationed at Chilliang Myntang, and detachments were sent to Nongjngi, Barato, Pungap and Kurwan. The left wing took its headquarters at Nongtalang with detachments at Iooksi, Padu and other areas. Operations were carried out simultaneously so that those who were at arms would not have any rest.[141]

On 11 December, 1862, an encounter at Jaintiapur was reported.[142] Attacks were also carried out at Jalong and surrounding villages were plundered.[143] On 23 December, the 21st Regiment Punjab Infantry under the command of Major Thelwall was attacked between Amwi and Jaintiapur. Casualties were reported on both the sides and the muskets and ammunitions of the *sepoys* killed were taken by the Jaintias.[144] Since the Regiment were accompanied with *coolies* carrying essential supplies, several *coolies* were wounded and killed.[145]

Capture and Execution of U Kiang Nangbah

U Kiang Nangbah and his most trusted lieutenant U Chey Rangbah toured the entire district to check and supervise the positioning of his men. The leaders who were working with U Kiang were U Long Padu, U Swar Sutnga, U Mon Rymbai, U Bang, U Bakher, U Mulon Mynso, U Kiang Sule, U Kat Changpung, and U Woh Riang.[146] Some Jaintias were passing information and working for the British because of the lure of money that was offered to them. Meanwhile U Kiang had taken ill and had retreated to Umkara. He sent his deputy U Che and others under him to go to Mynso to carry on the fight. He was looked after by his wife, Ka Miet Diat Khla Challam who had with her their two children, a son and a new born daughter.[147] The *Daloi* of Nartiang U Mon and his right hand man, U Long Sutnga[148] informed Lt. Sadlier about the place and state in which Kiang was in. On 27 December, 1862, a party under Lt. Sadlier, commanding the 28th Native Infantry at Nartiang led by U Long Sutnga a resident of Nartiang, effected the capture of U Kiang in the early hours of that day, but not without a resistance from U Kiang even though he was weakened from illness.

Sadlier in his letter to the Staff Officer of the Jaintia Field Force writes:[149]

> I arrived at the village in which Ookiang Nongba was making a sudden rush, I got into the village without my approach being observed, and at once got to the further side, being led in that direction by Oolong, the man who first gave me the information about the prisoner. My men now entered the house from all directions.... Oolong at the same time entered the house by the front door on which the prisoner came out into the back verandah of his house. With a view to jump into a jungly Koorung on the edge of which his house was built. On seeing me he went back into his house again.... Oolong, who, on seeing Ookiang Nongba at once rushed on him: the prisoner snapped a pistol in his face; he then took a double barrelled gun and pointed it at us. This also misfired ... on my coming up with the *sepoys* to help Oolong he at once fell back and then began defending himself with his sword ... seeing that he would not yield.... I ordered one of the men to fire on him; and another man, who had got into the verandah, to fix his bayonet. This being done, ... I called out 'put down your sword and I will not shoot you', this he did.... His wife and two children were taken prisoner, ... but she together with the children, escaped on the following night. In the village the sepoys caught nine other Jowai men.... To the Nurteng Dalloye and Oolong, I am indebted for the information which led to the capture of this noted rebel.

In Kiang's house six guns and a musket belonging to the 33rd Native Infantry Regiment was found.[150] U Kiang Nangbah was brought to trial before Brigadier Dunsford and Captain Morton the Deputy Commissioner.[151] On 30 December, 1862, he was hanged at 5.00 p.m. in the presence of the troops and all the villagers.[152] U Kiang throughout the trial remained indifferent though he was very much conscious that his life was at stake. Without behaving in a servile way for pardon he asked that his life would be spared for seven days. This was overruled by the military court and ordered out the "effect of severe measures".[153] U Kiang Nangbah was executed within three hours of his conviction[154] at Iawmusiang Jowai.[155]

The death of U Kiang Nangbah did not bring the uprising to an end. In the beginning of January 1863 the forces at Jowai comprising of the 21st Native Infantry Regiment under Major Thelwall and the Eurasian Battery of Artillery, under Captain Cordner was led by Colonel Dunsford to Umwai and then to Padu. Several stockades had again been erected in these places. Umkoi and Nongbarai was also visited by the troops. The stockades were destoryed, the Jaintias as usual took advantage of the dense forests.[156]

Military Operations Continue

Between 2 and 5 January, 1863, operations were carried out by Colonel Richardson with serious consequences. In the fight at Umkoi Colonel Richardson was wounded with a spear and a number of *sepoys* were wounded mortally.[157] Major Thelwall then took command and after some resistance the stockade was taken. The injured were taken to Padu. Richardson while attacking Umkrong was again badly injured close to the knee by a musket ball. This happened on 5 January. Major Thelwall took charge again and the stockade was destroyed. The number of injured *sepoys* in the second operation was high.[158] The troops under Robinson carried out their operations in Padu, Pomtadong and tried to drive the 'rebels' across the river Umngot into the Khyrim territory where they would be tracked down by Captain Macdonald, second in command of the Kamrup Regiment.[159] Since the destruction of these stockades, the Jaintias started to move through Khyriem state and made their way in the direction of Khyrwang and Nongphyllut on the borders of Assam. A meeting was held at Nongphyllut, where U Mulon, the former *Daloi* of Mynso, and the Principal leader after the execution of U Kiang Nangbah declared his determination to carry on the fight till the last. Other chiefs also proposed that they should hold out for another year.[160] There were also reports of encounters between "the Cossaya police under Captain Worsley and the Jaintias numbering around 3000 with women and children who have fortified themselves in a cave."[161]

In March 1863, expeditions were sent towards Barato and Nongphyllut in the north-eastern parts of Jaintia Hills chiefly by men of the 21st and 44th Regiment Native Infantry under the command of Major Thelwall.[162] The Punjabis and Gurkhas troops burned and plundered the villages. Grains were confiscated and those who were at arms were captured and killed, making the task easier for the British authorities.[163] Towards the end of March, many Jaintias had surrendered or returned to their villages except for the leaders who tried to persuade their people from doing the same. The majority of the people by this time had realized the futility of carrying out the fight particularly after the execution of U Kiang Nangbah. In the meeting at Nongphyllut the people who attended were in favour of returning back to their villages with their women and children. There were also cases where they were prevented by those who wanted to carry on the fight by leaders such as U Mulon and U Mon Lato. In the case of the latter, he prevented the people of Rymbai from tendering their submission but "infuriated by his oppression to their wishes, they slew him."[164]

By the month of April speculation was rife whether the "Little War in the Assam hills is, this time really at an end".[165] The attempts by the Jaintias to attack Nongbah was repulsed by the *Daloi* with his 80 supporters. U Bang the *Daloi* of Ralliang surrendered on condition that his life be spared. U Mulon, however, who was badly injured refused to come to terms.[166] The next three months that followed, army operation was suspended owing to incessant rains.

Between August and December 1863, operations were again carried out to apprehend those who were still at arms. But owing to the difficulty of moving about, and the dearth of information the authorities could not gain anything substantial. On 12 September, Hajjun Manik the Native Inspector captured two persons in arms. On 23 September, one of the rebel leaders was killed and another captured by him. At the end of the month 6 armed men were captured from Sutnga. They were charged of killing three villagers of Jowai in the previous month. On 20 October, the 'rebel' leader U Kiang Sarai surrendered at Jowai after having narrowly escaped capture two or three times. On 2 November, Inspector Hajjun Manik came on a party of Jaintias who were still at arms and were attacked heavily. In the process two Jaintias were killed and Bukhere, the leader escaped. On 11 November, Mulon surrendered and on 20 of the same month Bukhere with his followers gave themselves up to the authorities at Jowai.[167]

On 1 December, more Jaintias who had taken part in the resistance were captured from Sutnga. On 11 December U Kiang Bhein was captured.[168] U Sawar the *Daloi* of Sutnga was killed in an encounter with the troops. U Chey Rangbah, the lieutenant of U Kiang was killed in an encounter with the people of Nongbah. On 23 March, 1864, Haughton, the Commissioner, in his message to the Government of Bengal wrote: "the people have been very severely punished and that all inclination to rebel is at an end".[169] The losses of the troops and police employed in the suppression of the resistance of this last phase were very heavy.[170] The 44th Native Infantry which took part in the operations from first to last had four officers wounded in its various engagements.[171] The statistics about the other regiments is not available as the Government authorities were silent about the number of *sepoys* killed or wounded.

The uprising that rocked the entire Jaintia hills was finally suppressed towards the last part of 1863. This was achieved after considerable loss on both the sides as can be seen from the above discussions. U Kiang Nangbah's role in this struggle and his gallant adventures and exertions is still remembered by the people of Jaintia hills with great reverence. Though he was captured by an act of treason, his stand to the last has made him immortal. According to a tradition, U Kiang Nangbah before his execution told his people, who were forced by the troops to witness the scene, that after his death if his face turned east they would be free within one hundred years, and if it turned west they would remain captive forever. After he breathed his last, his face slowly turned towards the east.[172] True to his words, within one hundred years from the day he died, the British had to leave India.

REFERENCES

1. *The Englishman*, Wednesday, February 19, 1862; *The Friend of India*, 15 May, 1862.
2. Home Public Proceedings, 14 May, 1860, No. 134 1/2, Rowlatt to Jenkins.
3. Ibid.
4. Ibid.

5. Ibid.
6. Ibid.
7. Home Public Proceedings, 3 July, 1863, No. 30, J.C. Haughton to Secretary, Government of Bengal; P.N. Dutta, *Impact of the West on the Khasis and the Jaintias*, p. 88.
8. Home Public Proceedings, 14 May, 1860, No. 134[1]/2, Rowlatt to Jenkins.
9. Shobhan N. Lamare, "British Military Operations in the Jaintia Uprising of 1860: in *Proceedings of North-East India History Association*, 17th Session, p. 236; also in Home Public Proceedings, 14 May, 1860, No. 134½, Rowlatt to Jenkins.
10. Home Public Proceedings, 28 March, 1860, No. 30; Francis Jenkins to E.H. Lushington, Secretary to the Government of Bengal.
11. Home Public Proceedings, 19 May, 1860, No. 39/40(A); A.R. Young Esq., Secretary to the Government of Bengal to the Secretary, Government of India.
12. Home Public Proceedings, 14 May, 1860, No. 134½, Rowlatt to Jenkins.
13. Home Public Proceedings, 30 March, 1860, No. 31, Jenkins to E.H. Lushington; also in Shobhan N. Lamare, op. cit., p. 236.
14. Home Public Proceedings, 14 May, 1860, No. 134½, Rowlatt to Jenkins.
15. Home Public Proceedings, 11 April, 1860, No. 184; G.G. Balfour, Magistrate of Sylhet to the Commissioner of Circuit Dacca Division.
16. Home Public Proceedings, 14 May, 1860, No. 134½, Rowlatt to Jenkins.
17. Ibid.
18. Ibid.
19. Ibid.
20. Ibid.
21. Ibid.
22. Home Public Proceedings, 14 May, 1860, No. 134½; Rowlatt to Jenkins.
23. Ibid.
24. Ibid.
25. Ibid.
26. Home Public Proceedings, 14 May, 1860, No. 134½; Rowlatt to Jenkins.
27. Home Public Proceedings, 13 October, 1860, No. 59–81(A).
28. U Bnai ex-Daloi of Ralliang; U Kat former Pator of Ralliang; U Skam ex-Daloi of Shangpung; U Shan ex-Daloi of Shangpung; U Iong ex-Pator of Nongbah; U Mon ex-Daloi of Nartiang; U Long Sutna of Nartiang; U Iong ex-Daloi of Nangjngi; U Parbat u Rymbai; U Byong Songloo of Satpattor.
29. Home Public Proceedings, 23 May, 1860, No. 77; Francis Jenkins to A.R. Young, Secretary to the Government of India.
30. Ibid.
31. Ibid.
32. Ibid.
33. Home Public Proceedings, 23 May, 1860, No. 77; Francis Jenkins to A.R. Young, Secretary to the Government of India.
34. Home Public Proceedings, 13 October, 1860, No. 59–81(A).
35. *Selection of Records Government of Bengal* (henceforth *Selections*), 21 November 1861, No. 339½, Rowlatt to Henry Hopkinson.
36. *Selections* etc., 5 December, 1861, No. 691; Henry Hopkinson to Secretary, Government of Bengal.

37. *Selections* etc., Home Department, 3 January, 1862, No. 6(A), E.H. Lushington to Secretary, Government of India.
38. *Selections* etc., 16 January, 1862, No. 37; T. Smith to Commissioner of Circuit, Dacca Division.
39. Ibid.
40. Assam Secretariat Records, Commissioner's Papers, File No. 411 of 1863.
41. H. Bareh, *The History and Culture of the Khasi People*, pp. 166–167.
42. Assam Secretariat Records, Commissioner's Papers, File No. 411 of 1863.
43. J.B. Bhattacharjee, "The Jaintia Rebellion" in N.R. Ray (ed.), *Challenge*, p. 184.
44. This oral tradition is still very popular with the people and it is being held that the monument of U Kiang Nangbah stands today at a place where he was elected by the people as their leader. Interview with: O. Kyndiah, N. Sutnga, R. Nongtdu, H. Shylla and others.
45. Assam Secretariat Records, Commissioner's Papers, File No. 411 of 1863 also in J.B. Bhattacharjee, "The Jaintia Rebellion" in N.R. Ray (ed.), *Challenge*, p. 176.
46. D.R. Syiemlieh, *British Administration in Meghalaya and Pattern*, p. 90.
47. *Selections* etc., 9 April, 1862, Rowlatt to Secretary, Government of Bengal; also 21 January, 1862, Richardson to Adjutant General.
48. H. Bareh, *The History and Culture of the Khasi People*, p. 168.
49. *Selections* etc., 23 January, 1862, No. 49; T. Smith to Commissioner of the Dacca Division.
50. *Selections* etc., 20 January, 1862, No. 7; R. Abercrombie Officiating Commissioner of the Dacca Division to the Secretary, Government of Bengal.
51. *Selections* etc., 21 January, 1862, No. 43; T. Smith to the Commissioner of the Dacca Division.
52. *Selections* etc., 21 January, 1862, Richardson to Adjutant General; also in H.K. Barpujari, Problem of the Hill Tribes North-East Frontier 1843–1872, p. 77.
53. *Selections* etc., 21 January, 1862, No. 7; Richardson to Deputy Assistant General Presidency Division.
54. D.R. Syiemlieh, *British Administration in Meghalaya Policy and Pattern*, p. 90; also in *Selections* etc., 25 January, 1862, No. 52; T. Smith to the Commissioner of the Dacca Division.
55. *Selections* etc., 26 January, 1862, No. 574; M.H.J. Lance to Captain J. Hudson, Deputy Assistant Adjutant General.
56. Ibid.
57. *Selections* etc., 26 January, 1862, No. 9; Richardson to the Deputy Adjutant General.
58. *Selections* etc., 20 January, 1862, No. 10; Richardson to Assistant Adjutant General.
59. Ibid.
60. Ibid.
61. C.E. Buckland, Bengal under the Lietutenant Governors, Vol. I, pp. 180–182; Selections etc., 28 January, 1860, No. 15; R. Abercrombie, Officiating Commissioner of Dacca Division to the Secretary, Government of Bengal.

62. *Selections* etc., 9 February, 1862, No. 12; Richardson to Assistant Adjutant General.
63. Ibid.
64. *Selections* etc., 11 February, 1862, No. 13; Richardson to Assistant Adjutant General.
65. *Selections* etc., 15 February, 1862, No. 14; Richardson to Assistant Adjutant General.
66. *Selections* etc., 20 February, 1862, No. 18; Richardson to Assistant Adjutant General.
67. Home Public Proceedings, 23 February, 1862, Rowlatt to Hopkinson.
68. *Selections* etc., 25 February, 1862, No. 2; Captain R.G. Chambers to Assistant Adjutant General.
69. *Selections* etc., 15 March, 1862, No. 27; Hopkinson to E.H. Lushington.
70. Home Public Proceedings, 23 February, 1862, No. 15; Rowlatt to Hopkinson.
71. *Selections* etc., 4 March, 1862, No. 15(A), Rowlatt to Hopkinson.
72. *Selections* etc., 14 March, 1862; Robinson to Dunsford.
73. *Selections* etc., 14 March, 1862, No. 30; Richardson to Assistant Adjutant General.
74. *Selections* etc., 22 March, 1862, No. 32; Hopkinson to Lushington.
75. *Selections* etc., 22 March, 1862, No. 32; Hopkinson to Lushington.
76. Ibid.
77. Ibid.
78. *Selections* etc., 15 March, 1862, No. 41, Jynteahpore; Dunsford to Assistant Adjutant General.
79. *Selections* etc., 19 March, 1862, No. 30; Lt. Herbert Sconce, Deputy Commissioner Nowgong to H. Hopkinson.
80. *Selections* etc., 25 March, 1862, No. 18; Hopkinson to Showers.
81. Home Public Proceedings, 12 April, 1862, Nos. 100–101; Dunsford to Assistant Adjutant General.
82. *Selections* etc., 22 March, 1862, No. 34(A); Showers to Adjutant General of the Army.
83. *Selections* etc., 26 March, 1862, No. 795(A); E.H. Lushington, Secretary, Government of Bengal to Commissioner of Assam. Also in *The Englishman*, May 13, 1862.
84. *Selections* etc., 28 March, 1862, Grey to Lushington.
85. *Selections* etc., 2 April, 1862, No. 885(A); Lushington to Showers.
86. *Selections* etc., 31 May, 1862, Showers to the Secretary, Government of Bengal.
87. *Selections* etc., 4 February, 1863, Haughton to Secretary, Government of Bengal.
88. Ibid.
89. *Selections* etc., 2 April, 1862, No. 63; Dunsford to Assistant Adjutant General.
90. *Selections* etc., 2 April, 1862, No. 63; Dunsford to Assistant Adjutant General.
91. *Selections* etc., 7 April, 1862, No. 979(A); J.P.H. Ward, Officiating Under Secretary to the Government of Bengal, to the Commissioner of Assam.

92. D.R. Syiemlieh, *British Administration in Meghalaya, Policy and Pattern,* p. 91.
93. *Selections* etc., 15 April, 1862, No. 2; Showers to the Government of Bengal.
94. Bengal Judicial Proceedings, September, 1813, Nos. 153–155.
95. Assam Secretariat Records, Commissioner's Paper, File No. 411 of 1863.
96. Home Public Proceedings, 24 July, 1862, No. 51(B); Morton to the Secretary, Government of Bengal.
97. Ibid.
98. *The Friend of India,* 15 May, 1862 and 3 July, 1862; Home Public Proceedings, 24 July, 1862, No. 51(B); A. Andrew to Morton; also in D.R. Syiemlieh, op. cit., p. 93.
99. Home Public Proceedings, 24 July, 1862, No. 51(B); A. Andrew to Morton.
100. Ibid.
101. Ibid.
102. Assam Secretariat Records Commissioner's Paper, File No. 411 of 1863.
103. Home Public Proceedings, 19 June, 1862, Nos. 56–57(B); Morton to Secretary, Government of Bengal.
104. H. Bareh, *The History and Culture of the Khasi People,* p. 172.
105. *Selections* etc., 18 November, 1862, No. 2524; A. Eden, Secretary to the Government of Bengal to the Commissioner of Assam.
106. Home Public Proceedings, 15 August, 1862, No. 59–61; J.C. Haughton to B.W.D. Morton.
107. Ibid.
108. Home Public Proceedings, 22 August, 1862, No. 59–61, Gowhatty; Haughton to Morton.
109. Ibid.
110. Ibid.
111. *Selections* etc., 28 August 1862, No. 278; Morton to Haughton.
112. *The Englishman,* Wednesday, February, 19, 1862.
113. Ibid.
114. Ibid.
115. Ibid.
116. Home Public Proceedings, 30 August, 1862, No. 51; J.D. Gordon to B.W.D. Morton.
117. *Selections* etc., 28 August, 1862, No. 278; Morton to Haughton.
118. Ibid.
119. Home Public Proceedings, 8 September, 1862, No. 59–61(A); Gordon to Haughton.
120. *Selections* etc., 1 October, 1862; Morton to the Commissioner of Assam.
121. B.J.P. November 1862, No. 352; *Selections* etc., 20 October, 1862, No. 32, Haughton to the secretary, Government of Bengal.
122. *Selections* etc., 4 January, 1863; Haughton to the Secretary, Government of Bengal.
123. *Selections* etc., 20 October, 1862, No. 32; Haughton to the Secretary, Government of Bengal.
124. *Selections* etc., Ibid., also in H.K. Barpujari, Problem of the Hill tribes, North-East Frontier 1843–1872, p. 82.

125. *Selections* etc., 12 November, 1862, No. 17(C); Haughton to the Secretary, Government of Bengal; also in Q. Sumer, *U Kiang Nangbah* (in Khasi), p. 15.
126. *Selections* etc., 15 October, 1862; Morton to the Secretary, Government of Bengal.
127. Ibid.
128. *Selections* etc., 27 October, 1862; Morton to Secretary, Government of Bengal.
129. J.H. Thornton, *Memories of Seven Campaigns*, p. 95.
130. Home Public Proceedings, 7 November, 1862, No. 41–44(A), Morton to Secretary, Government of Bengal.
131. *Selections* etc., 12 November, 1862, No. 17(C); Haughton to the Secretary, Government of Bengal.
132. J.H. Thorton, op. cit., p. 116.
133. Ibid.
134. *Selections* etc., 18 November, 1862, No. 2524; A. Eden to Commissioner of Assam; also in Home Public Proceedings, 18 November, 1862, No. 43(A).
135. *Selections* etc., 18 November, 1862, No. 2524; A. Eden to Commissioner of Assam.
136. D.R. Syiemlieh, op. cit., p. 93; Abstracts of Letters from India, 1863, Narratives of the Government of Bengal, No. 64, pp. 50–57.
137. *The Friend of India*, October 1862.
138. *Selections* etc., 28 October 1862; Morton to the Secretary, Government of Bengal.
139. Home Public Proceedings, 2 December, 1862, No. 34(A); Telegraph Message, Morton to Secretary, Government of Bengal.
140. *Selections* etc., 1 December, 1862, No. 452; Captain Gilbert to Dunsford.
141. Ibid.
142. Home Public Proceedings, 22 December, 1862, No. 38(A); Telegraph Message, Morton to Secretary to the Government of Bengal.
143. Home Public Proceedings, 22 December, 1862, No. 49–50(A); Telegraph Message, Morton to Secretary, Government of Bengal.
144. *Selections* etc., 25 September, 1862, No. 400; Major Thelwall to Dunsford.
145. Ibid.
146. Q. Sumer, op. cit., p. 17.
147. Op. cit., p. 18.
148. *Selections* etc., 3 January, 1863, Walcott to Morton.
149. *Selections* etc., 29 December, 1862; Lt. Sadlier to the Staff Officer of the Jynteah Field Force Camp Jowai.
150. Ibid.
151. *Selections* etc., 6 January, 1863, Morton to Haughton.
152. *Selections* etc., 31 December, 1862; Dunsford to Captain Gilbert, Assistant Adjutant General.
153. Ibid.
154. Ibid.
155. Q. Sumer, op. cit., p. 20.
156. J.H. Thornton, op. cit., pp. 117–118.
157. Op. cit., p. 120; also in *Selections* etc., 6 January, 1863, Morton to Haughton.

158. J.H. Thornton, op. cit., p. 120; also in the *Friend of India,* 15 January 1863.
159. *Selections* etc., 6 January, 1863; Morton to Haughton.
160. *The Friend of India,* 2 February, 1863.
161. Op. cit., 26 February, 1863.
162. J.H. Thornton, op. cit., p. 125.
163. *The Friend of India,* 5 March, 1863.
164. Op. cit., 26 March, 1863.
165. Op. cit., 9 April, 1863.
166. Op. cit.
167. Home Public Proceedings, 21 December, 1863, No. 71; Lt. Worsley to Major H. Raban, Inspector General of Police, Assam Circle.
168. Ibid.
169. B.J.P. April, 1863, No. 460; also in H.K. Barpujari, *Problem of the Hill Tribes North-East Frontier 1843–1872,* Vol. II, p. 86.
170. J.H. Thornton, op. cit., p. 126.
171. Ibid.
172. J.B. Bhattacharjee, "The Jaintia Rebellion" in N.R. Ray (ed.), *Challenge,* p. 185.

5

The Aftermath of Resistance

Active military operations against the Jaintias drew to a close in December 1863, by which time a majority of the people who were at arms were either killed in encounters or captured. The British in order to instill fear and to impose their authority on those who dared to rebel set an example by trying 'offenders' under Act XI of 1857. Under provision of this Act many Jaintias were tried and some were transported for life. In this context it may be mentioned that some were also hanged, their crime-rebelling against the British Government. The case of "Oossa Maratteang" of Rymbai may also be referred to here. He was tried by Captain B.W.D. Morton on 16 January 1863 and was sentenced to be "hung by the neck till he be dead".[1]

The policy of bringing the entire tract of Jaintia Hills under the control of the British authorities was made possible because of the "early fall or capture of all the rebel chiefs".[2] The *Syiem* of Khyriem Rabon Sing was also instrumental in bringing those who had challenged the British authority to come out of their hideouts and to surrender on condition that their lives would be spared.

Morton's Proposals

In 1862, while the struggle was still intense, the Deputy Commissioner, Khasi and Jaintia Hills, Captain B.W.D. Morton had suggested certain measures "as to the future settlement of the district and the system upon which its affairs in all departments *i.e.*, Judicial, Revenue and Police" should be carried out.[3] The suggestions that he had referred to, were an extension on the reports of A.J.M. Mills and W.J. Allen.

Allen in speaking of the administration of justice in Jaintia Hills had dealt at length with the chances in which the Jaintia people would obtain justice at the hands of their chiefs. In paragraph 253 and 255 he observes: "the first step towards a reform in the administration of public affairs in the 15 Dolloyeship ought, I think, to be to abolish at once the office of Pathor, and to strictly prohibit any interference on the part of the Langdeos in Judicial matters; there should be no vicarious agency."[4] Allen wanted that all the duties of each Daloiship should be discharged by the *Daloi* himself in persons. He pointed out:[5]

> The great curse of the present system is that there are so many expensive, corrupt, fruitless and unnecessary investigations and decisions even in the smallest matters. In the Mofussils, in each Illaqua, there ought to be only one authority and one decision; what is done there should be done by one Dolloye and one Durbar; then at all events, whatever may be the result, whether the aggrieved finds justice or meets with additional wrong, there will be only one Dolloye to propitiate and one Durbar to bribe; there will be no waste of time; no mockery of justice before a greedy deputy and a grasping village priest.

In the light of the above, Morton suggested that a sub-division in the Jaintia Hills under a Military Assistant Commissioner should be established. Jowai was recommended as site for such a sub-division by the earlier reports, but he was of the opinion that it was not sufficiently centrical and therefore preferred the Ralliang *Elaka* should be selected.[6] In the judicial field he added that the powers held by the *Dalois* of adjucating petty and criminal suits should be withdrawn and suitors should refer to the Assistant Commissioner stationed at Ralliang. Morton emphasized that the people should be taught to look to the Government officers for justice. The Assistant should hold the powers of a First Class Subordinate Magistrate and Sudder Ameen. No agent or counsel under any pretence, should be admitted in the Jaintia court and the proceedings should be carried out in the simplest manner, excepting in heinous cases, not exceeding the powers of the Deputy Commissioner would be taken down by the Assistant in English and forwarded for orders. It would remain, however, optional with the Deputy Commissioner to summon the parties to his court.[7] He also suggested that "all heinous cases should be heard by the Deputy Commissioner".[8] In case of appeals both in civil and criminal cases that would arise from the order of the Assistant Commissioner should lie at the Deputy Commissioner's office in Shillong.[9]

As to matters relating to revenue, the Deputy Commissioner was of the opinion that the collection of the same should be carried out by the *Dalois*. It may be recalled that the order limiting the authority of the *Dalois* was passed in 1841, and triennial elections were held in 1850, but the latter's order did not appear to have ever been fully carried out. Both these grievances were mentioned by U Don to W.J. Allen in 1858. U Don was of the opinion that he paid Rs. 380 for his office and having to pay for his re-election once in three years was burdeonsome. The statement made by U Don appears that he had paid Rs. 350 to the *Muktear* of the late Henry Inglis, son-in-law of the then Political Agent; a gold *Mohur* to Solomon the interpreter and Rs. 15 to Ram Mohun the treasurer, in order to ensure his appointment as the *Daloi* of Jowai.[10] It was due to these allegations that B.W.D. Morton the Deputy Commissioner came up with a suggestion, that the *Dalois* should be selected by the people and their appointments should be for life. This appointment on the other hand, to be liable for cancelled by the Deputy Commissioner if the *Daloi* was found to be indulging in other forms of malpractices. Since the *Daloi* would be given the responsibility of collecting the revenues, a commission of twenty percent from the revenue collected would be given as compensation for the work carried out by him. The *Dalois* were to be furnished with printed receipts for distribution to those from whom the revenue was collected. The revenues of Jaintia Hills would be decided by the Government in communication with the Governor-General's Agent stationed at Gauhati. The revenue that was collected would be forwarded by the same authority to Government and not through the Comissioner to the Board of Revenue as it used to be.[11]

Regarding the role of the police force, Morton was of the opinion that at least for some years it would be necessary for the Government to keep a larger regular force in the hills. He was convinced that troops should be stationed at both Jowai and Ralliang and that they must be under the command of European officers. In the case of the former he suggested that 150 men should be placed and in the case of the latter 250 men would be sufficient enough in maintaining law and order. Apart from the above two places, the police would also be stationed in small numbers at other stations such as Nangjngi, Nongfloot and Amwi.[12]

Educating the Jaintias was another consideration for the British authorities. Captain Morton stressed on the need to educate the Jaintias. The Welsh missionaries by this period had already made their settlement at Jowai but because of the uprising the activities of the missionaries had been affected. It was expected that once law and order were established the missionaries would continue their work once again. Along with English schools, Bengali schools were also recommended in the sub-division headquarter *i.e.*, at the Ralliang *elaka*. Morton wanted this to be some kind of an experiment and if it was successful, more schools in the similar pattern would be opened.[13] The Deputy Commissioner also stressed on the need of communication and this problem, according to him, "should be attended by the government at the earliest"[14] It was proposed that the district and sub-division headquarters should be connected with each other and the several police stations. He remarked: "to do the hills justice an executive officer in the settlement of the country be deputed to Jowai .... His attention should first be turned to the bridging of the rivers over which his roads will pass. A road without bridges is useless, whereas with rivers made passable troops could move all over the hills. There is a fair road between Cherrapoonjee and Jowai but for want of bridge across the Mungot, communication is closed for days at a time."[15]

Hopkinson's Note

Henry Hopkinson, Agent to the Governor-General North-East Frontier in a communication to the Secretary, Government of Bengal proposed to introduce a system of assessment that was in vogue in Burma at that time. He wanted that poll tax and land tax should be introduced, and "land in cultivation should be assessed or in respect to which a private proprietary right was asserted, at one rupee an acre and a poll tax of one rupee a head on every male between the age of 16 and 60."[16] Hopkinson, however, was against the operation of the income tax. He stated, "it is a tax utterly unsuited to such a people".[17]

Shower's Suggestion

More suggestion on Jaintia hills were put forward by Brigadier-General ST.G.D. Showers. In this correspondence to the Secretary to the Government of Bengal, Shower pointed out that "the British Government on the transfer of the district to their authority continued the administration as it had been conducted by the former government until the receipt of the House tax which was very trifling".[18] It would appear therefore, that the British Government had never received any revenue from the Jaintia people and Shower's was not in favour that the government should receive any.[19] He also pointed out that there was no institution or establishment in Jaintia Hills by which the people would benefit and which would justify the imposition of a tax. According to him, the people are "too ignorant and savage to understand the meaning of it and they are too poor to bear the burden of imposition. The general rules that are applicable to the wealthier and more advanced provinces of the empire are not adapted for this uncivilized race, and they should not be applied to them."[20] He recommended that the income tax should be abolished by law in the district. Regarding the house tax he was also in favour of its abolition, but in consequence of the uprising he wanted the same to continue and to be kept for the future as a royalty.[21] Suggestions were also put forward that a civil officer should be stationed at Jowai to supervise the native element and who would be entrusted with greater judicial and police powers.[22]

Prior to these developments in April 1862, the income tax that was assessed throughout the Jaintia Hills fetched the sum of rupees 1,259. The chart below gives details.[23]

Income Tax in Jynteah Hills

Places	Persons		Rate	Rs	As	P	Total
Jowai*	1	×	5	5	0	0	
Jowai*	18	×	4–8	81	0	0	= 302
Jowai*	54	×	4	216	0	0	
Nurteng	37	×	4	148	0	0	= 148
Nungba	4	×	4–8	18	0	0	= 138
Nungba	30	×	4	120	0	0	
Ralliong*	32	×	4	128	0	0	= 128
Sathpoonjee*	26	×	4	104	0	0	= 104
Nongjoongee	25	×	4	100	0	0	= 100
Munsow*	17	×	4	68	0	0	= 68
Nongfloot*	17	×	4	68	0	0	= 68
Shamphong*	16	×	4	64	0	0	= 64
Rumbai*	10	×	4	40	0	0	= 40
Amwai*	1	×	9	9	0	0	= 31
Amwai*	5	×	4–8	22	0	0	
Shilliong-Muntang	6	×	4	24	0	0	= 24
Sathpathor	6	×	4	24	0	0	= 24
Satongah*	5	×	4	20	0	0	= 20

Note: (a) Those marked with an asterisk rebelled, the others did not.
(b) The highest rate levied was rupees 9, which was paid by the Daloi of Amwi. Only one person paid rupees 5, twenty-seven persons Rs. 4–8 and the rest numbering 281, Rs. 4 each, the total number of the persons assessed to the tax being therefore 310.

With the pacification of the hills and the revival of trade and commerce, Shower in order to cover the expenses of such improvements suggested that taxes may be laid down in some indirect ways. These, he suggested might take the form of toll taxes on roads and bridges which the people would be using for their advantage.

After the military operations the question on administrating the country came up for discussion, whether the officers in charge of the district should be from the military department, vested with civil charge or whether he should be purely a civil officer. Regarding this, Showers was of the opinion that it should be in line with the political agencies of Shimla and Dehradun and therefore, in this context Jaintia hills should come under the civil amdinistration.[24] Since in the hills the *Dalois* were the heads of the political institutions, he was in favour of retaining this office and the *Dalois* were to continue in office, once elected for a period of three years in accordance to the rules that was then in force. He suggested that the appointments, instead of being vacated at the end of the term, should only be reconsidered. This would be subjected to a change if the village community or the officers in charge of the district were dissatisfied with the activities of the *Dalois,* where fresh elections would then be called for. The jurisdiction of the *Dalois* were to remain and stay as they were before. They were to try all cases within a certain amount and to levy fines as they used to do. If the *Daloi* was found indulging in any kind of malpractices and if it were proved he would be summarily dismissed. Since the *Daloi* at that time were largely illiterate like most of the villagers, Showers proposed that arrangements should be made to encourage them to learn how to read and write. In order to give incentives in this aspect, it was further argued that, if the *Daloi* can read his own decisions, they would be conferred with higher powers. This might be extended from time to time till he would be vested with the jurisdiction of a *Moonsiff* or a *Sudder Ameen.* The *Daloi* was to be assisted in his activities by the *Sangots* and *Wasans* and he would also be at the head of the police. The *Daloi* was also to send daily reports to the Assistant in charge of the Division by a *Sangot* or any other person.[25] As for their pay, the amount which the *Daloi* realised from their village land would be kept by them. As and when the Dalois would qualify themselves for the exercise of the powers of *Sudder Ameen* then the Government would decide whether a government salary should be granted to them or not.[26]

As part of their confidence building measures that were carried out, Showers opined that there might be every possibility for the *Daloi* to collude with the people and try to withheld reports, but he insisted that "it is better to commence with a system of confidence and to secure the integrity of officers by means of a moral influence than by the institutions of checks and restrictions." At the same time he added that if a *Daloi* was convicted in any kind of fraud or deception he should be dismissed from his office.[27]

It may be recalled that earlier W.J. Allen in his report relevant to the administration of the Jaintia Hills, recommended that the office of the *Pators*, the deputy of the *Daloi*, should be abolished. Showers on the other hand, was in favour of retaining this office on the ground that "he is simply the assistant to the Dolloye and exercised no independent power".[28] It was also seen during that period, that in large villages where the *Dalois* does not reside, the *Langdoh* exercise judicial authority in minor cases, and Showers was also in favour of retaining the same, and if required the *Langdoh* should act as the superior police officer in the village and to send his reports by the *Sangot* to the *Daloi*. The number of officials like the *Sangots*, the *Wasans* and other petty officers were to be fixed by the *Daloi's* subjects to the approval of the Superintendent under the recommendation of the Assistant.

Regarding trade and commerce as well as cultivation, Showers noted that the hills abounded in limestone quarries and coal mines. Works in the mines were carried out by the Europeans alone and the natives would engage themselves as daily labourers. As for cultivation he suggested that apart from rice, other grains including wheat and vegetables should be introduced. A sanatorium at some places would serve the purpose he added. With the district being annexed to some Commissioner's divisions the *Sudder* station of the division would be in the hills and these developments would attract trade and population and would call out more rapidly the resources of the district. Showers was also emphasising that a contingent allowance should be sanctioned on application, for the purchase of implements for industrial pursuits. He recommended a pit saw as an implement which would be useful where the people would use the same to their own advantage.[29]

The last subject on which he gave equal importance was the spread of education. According to him, the people of Jaintia Hills "have no prejucide against receiving from European teachers either secular or religious instructions. Their feelings are free and open and they are prepared to learn either through the medium of the Bengalee or the Roman character."[30] The school that had been set up by Rev. Thomas Jones, taught the people about the first rudimentary form of learning, basically the three R's (reading, writing and arithmetic). Bengali schools were also recommended by Showers especially for those people who were having transactions in other districts. It was also expected that the Superintendent would submit a statement of the number of schools that might be established with the probability of their being attended.

Haughton's Recommendation

Lieutenant Colonel J.C. Haughton, Officiating Agent, Governor-General North-East Frontier recommended certain measures as to the general administration of Jaintia Hills after the suppression of the resistance. According to him, if peace were to be maintained in the entire territory, then two options are open: either to leave the people in their old state and not to interfere in their activities or to increase the intercourse of the British with them and by real government to introduce civilization and order among them.[31] He suggested an English officer be stationed in Jowai or in any other place which was convenient, to be subject to the chief authority in the hills and whose decisions would be final. However, reservations might be made that sentences in cases of a heinous nature and involving long periods of imprisonment or where life is at stake should be confined by the Lieutenant-Governor. For the management of the affairs in the village a *Panchayat* form of organisation was proposed where a *Sardar* or a headman would preside. His other duty would be to collect revenue and to apprehend offenders. The *Panchayat* would also look into any kind of grievance that might arise within the village and to refer to the higher authorities if crimes were committed or if there was dispute in which the people of two villages might be concerned. This village *Panchayat* would be formed by the people. The headman would receive a *Sunnad* but his appointment would be subjected to the confirmation of the officer incharge of the district.[32]

Regarding the case of the *Dalois,* Haughton was of the opinion that he would allow any number of villages not less than two, to elect their own *Daloi,* but again, his election to office would be subjected to confirmation of the officer who was incharge of the district, by whom a *sunnad* would be granted. The appointment of the *Daloi* was to be during good behaviour and he could be removed with the sanction of the chief officer in the hills. As to the fines that were collected by the *Dalois,* Haughton was in favour of the traditional method where the village authorities and the *Dalois* were to impose and to share the fines among themselves. The *Sardar* was to collect the revenue under the supervision of the *Daloi* and both would receive a liberal percentage of 25 per cent from the amount as compensation for their troubles in collecting it and for police duty.[33]

In the judicial department, Haughton preferred that the officer in charge of the district should refrain from interfering in those cases which are decided by the village council and the *Dalois*. The officer could only do so if he was convinced that obvious injustice was apparent. The proceedings in the court of the chief officer of the district would be in English and no *Mukteers* was to be allowed on any pretence. This again would not mean that the *Raja* would not be allowed to send his representatives. The people could name any persons to decide their case in the *Panchayats* if they so preferred and the village authorities could prevent anyone from doing so.

For the Police force he had this to say:[34]

> There should I think, be no police force as the term is ordinarily understood. The officer incharge of the district might have eight or ten *Chapprasies,* whose business it would be to carry messages to the *Dalois* and etc. and to see that any order for the capture of criminals or otherwise was carried into effect. The officer should also have a sufficient number of local *sepoys,* whether called police or not, at his own disposal for his protection and to enable him to arrest any offender who might defy the local authorities.

The village system though according to him was "not the very best"[35] yet he was convinced that it would be the "most expedient"[36] for some more years to come. The *Pators,* the *Langdohs,* the *Sangots* and others could act as village council which was again subject to the general authority of the *Dalois*.

In the field of education, Haughton suggested that a government school to give instruction in Bengali should be opened at Jowai. The objective was to encourage the sons of the more respectable and well to do, to attend the school. The Welsh Presbyterian Mission was to be encouraged to open as many schools as possible in order to emphasize more on vernacular form of education and for this, grants-in-aid would be made available so that the same could be carried out effectively.[37]

Haughton had also seen the importance of having roads. An estimate for a road through the hills had already been placed before the Lieutenant Governor. This road, however, did not pass through Jaintia Hills but lay twenty miles from its frontier and therefore, could not materially benefit the people. During that time the only principal route through Jaintia was the one which ran from Jaintiapur to Jowai and Jagi in the Nowgong district of Assam.[38] This route was put in order by David Scott in 1829, but was never completed. It was owing to this that he suggested that every new road should, if possible be laid out by a person of experience in that business. He remarked: "It is absolutely indispensable to the proper construction of what Government had undertaken, and that an experienced officer in the department of public works should be appointed with no other duty, but that of their superintendence".[39]

As to the Income Tax and the Stamp Act he categorically stated that they should never have been extended to the Jaintia Hills for these were measures that could be introduced only in civilized countries.[40]

End of Operations

Though active military operations had been suspended by March 1863, the troops stationed in the hills were not withdrawn till confidence was thoroughly restored.[41] The Secretary to the Government of Bengal, E.H. Lushington in his communication to Lieutenant Colonel J.C. Haughton mentions that unless "the people are convinced that they can rely upon the Government and its civil officers, for the protection of their lives and property, and prompt redress to their grievances, it would be unwise to withdraw any of the troops that are now stationed in the hills."[42] Lushington preferred that the 44th and the 21st Native Infantry Regiments along with the 1st battalion of the Bengal Military Police should be retained in the hills and their presence in the hills would suffice any kind of military purposes there. It was also felt that the services of the 28th Native Infantry Regiment could be dispensed with and the Kamrup Regiment to be broken up and incorporated into the police force. By the end of 1864 it was expected that the services of one of the three remaining regiments might be done away with. It was also believed that if the police of the Jaintia Hills be eventually left in the hands of the people themselves, under their own village chief, the strength of the organized police might again be reduced. All these were proposals for the later phase, but for the time being any kind of reduction in the strength of the force was considered to be inexpedient. The rapid concentration of troops in 1860 and the consequent discomfiture of the Jaintias were events of too recent date for the authorities to forget.[43] The successful suppression of the events of 1860 had led the authorities to reduce the strength of the regiment of Colonel Richardson from 1,200 to 600 *sepoys*. On the other hand, the Jaintia chiefs thinking that the reduction in the strength of the *sepoys* was an indication of the weakness of the British Government had risen and challenged the British again.[44]

Meanwhile the authorities in Calcutta decided to follow a policy of interaction with the Jaintia and not "to leave them in their old state".[45] While adopting a simple plan of governance it was decided that it should be suitable to their present condition and interfering as little as possible with existing institutions. The main idea behind this was to extend the interaction with the people and to introduce new thoughts and ideas.

New Administrative Structure

The proposal of Haughton of stationing an English officer at Jowai or in any other place which would be more convenient was accepted by the authorities in Calcutta. The officer would act as an Assistant Commissioner exercising powers in criminal cases and under the general provisions of the code of criminal procedure. He would have full power of a Magistrate incharge of a sub-division and in civil cases the powers of a *Sudder Ameen*. In the police department he would have the powers of a Magistrate, limited by the provisions of Act No. V of 1861.[46] In revenue and other matters the officers would exercise the ordinary jurisdiction of an officer in-charge of a sub-division. The general control of the district, however, would remain as it was with the Deputy Commissioner in charge of the Khasi and Jaintia Hills. The officers while exercising a concurrent authority in all matters with the Assistant Commissioner were also empowered to take up and dispose off cases. They would also occupy the place of the court of session, under the code of criminal procedure and act as a court of appeal in civil cases. The Judicial Commissioner of Assam would exercise the powers of the High Court in respect to cases relating to Jaintia Hills under the provision of Act XV of 1862.[47]

The arrangements of 1863 saw some more changes on the role of the *Dalois* and their responsibilities towards their own village or *Elaka*. It was suggested that every village or *Elaka* should have a *Daloi* or *Sardar*, chosen by the people, but their appointment to these posts could be subject to the confirmation of the Assistant Commissioner and not removable. The *Daloi* could be removed only on grounds of misconduct or in efficiency in carrying out the activities assigned to him. The *Daloi* was to be assisted by the *Pators* or the *Langdohs* whenever necessary and these officials would constitute the *Panchayat*. These officers would be appointed by the Assistant Commissioner in accordance with the wishes of the people to be ascertained either by elections or otherwise and to occupy their offices during good behaviour. The number of *Pators* and *Langdohs* required in each village or *Elaka* would be determined by the Assistant Commissioner. If any *Elaka* was too big, it would be sub-divided and formed into two or more *Elakas*. These newly formed *Elakas* would then be under a separate *Daloi* and their duties to be performed by the *Panchayat* as a body, or by each members separately, would have to be clearly defined.

The *Dalois* were held responsible for the police of their several villages or *Elakas*. The action of the organised police was restricted only to the suppression of any form of disturbances and to support the *Dalois* if their authorities were restricted. The Dalois with the assistance of the *Panchayat* would try criminal and civil cases except those of heinous crimes or relating to people from other villages or persons other than Jaintias. The Assistant Commissioner was empowered to call up any criminal trial or civil cases and to decide it by himself. The proceedings in the *Panchayat* and in the court of the *Daloi* would remain *viva voce* and no records were to be maintained of them.[48] In the case of the proceedings before the Assistant Commissioner both in the civil and criminal cases it should be oral, and a brief record thereof taken down by the Assistant Commissioner in English in his own handwriting.

For the collection of revenues, the *Dalois* in each village or *Elaka* were given the responsibility of collecting the same and a remuneration not exceeding 20 per cent from what was collected was given for the trouble he had taken. The practice of sharing the fines imposed by the members of the panchayats was discontinued. The *Dalois* or *Sardars* of every village were required to attend before the Assistant Commissioner not less than once a month and in case of inability to attend, one of the members of the *Panchayat* had to be sent for the said purpose. It was also expected that the Assistant Commissioner would establish a friendly and confidential understanding with the members and to move about frequently to every village within his jurisdiction, at least once a year.[49] Instructions were also given to the officers that they should make themselves masters over the Khasi language so as to be able to communicate freely.[50] Steps were also taken in the Public Works Department to appoint special officers for the construction of hill roads. The construction of minor roads was given to other civil officers but they were again under the supervision of the special officer appointed in the Public Works Department. As part of their confidence building measures, the authorities from Bengal issued clear instructions to the officers working in these hills that no persons should be excluded from office merely on account of the part he may have taken in the revolt.[51]

Accordingly, Captain Clarke assumed office as Assistant Commissioner of the Jaintia Hills Sub-Division, the geographical limits of which was defined much later by a notification on 16 November 1869.[52] Between the last part of 1863 and early 1864, it was noticed by the authorities that the settlement of the country had progressed rapidly. These developments had enabled the government to withdraw all the troops with the exception of two regiments of the Native Infantry which were permanently stationed in the hills,[53] till 1885 when the charge of the protection of the sub-division was handed over to the civil police.[54] The special commission appointed under Act XI of 1857 for the trial of offenders was also dissolved, and the ordinary criminal courts soon resumed their functions.[55] The Board of Revenue likewise resumed their authority in revenue matters throughout the district.[56]

The Assistant Commissioner was hopeful that the military campaigns that was carried against the Jaintias would have some kind of influence on their ethos. The military operations that were carried out by the 21st Regiment Punjab Native Infantry, the 44th Regiment Native Infantry, the Artillery Company and others, no doubt had serious overtones. The killings and destruction that was carried out in the countryside, where houses, belongings and crops were burnt and plundered, and in some cases attempts to starve the people by closing down the *hats* in the frontier, had tremendous influence on the people. Though initially these were the factors that made the people adamant and stubborn in their resistance; in the long run the measures which the British had carried out proved to be otherwise. The atrocities that were committed by the Nowgong Militia[57] where heads of the so called "rebels" were severed and sent to their commandants as trophies[58] had much to say on the barbaric acts on the part of some of the British army personnel.[59] The measures that were carried out in flushing those in arms against the British authorities, from the jungles, resulted in the killings of innocent lives, where sometimes even women were included and their families captured.[60] It is believed that, it was because of these measures that some of the chiefs decided to mediate for a compromise. This was not without a heavy price. Those who were in arms looked at those chiefs as traitors who were siding with the British for their own selfish interest. Some lost their lives in the process. In order to instill fear and to speed up trials Act No. XI of 1857 was applied to the Jaintia Hills by which a large number of people who were at arms were sentenced. There were also cases of transportation for life. The cases of Mullon and Bukhere may be referred to. The British records do not indicate the place where they were sent for transportation. The details of those tried and the nature of sentences can be seen from Charts A (1862), B (1863), C (1863), and D (1863), enclosed at the end of this chapter.

It appears that some men who were sentenced were sent to Cherra jails but there were cases also, when they were confined in the Quarter Guard. It is not known whether these people were brought back to Jaintia Hills or not after serving their sentences. In this context, it may be mentioned that quite a number of Jaintias who had converted to Christianity were removed to Cherrapunji with the commencement of the outbreak when their settlement was attacked and burnt. In this case too, British records do not provide any information whether they were asked to go back after the pacification of the hills or whether other arrangements were made for them to settle there. The presence today of a number of Jaintia clans in Cherrapunji, perhaps, would subscribe to the above assertion that at one stage or the other these people might have been victims of circumstances and were taken to that part of the country and preferred to stay on.

The Jaintia Rajas Position

The Jaintia resistance affected the position of the former Jaintia Raja. Major Rowlatt was first of the opinion that at one stage or the other, the *Raja* might had formented the uprising and "that he merely withdrew himself from the disturbance he had caused when he found that the rebellion was imminent".[61] To this Haughton disagreed and pointed out that the 'rebels' were disappointed when the *Raja* refused to lead them in their struggle and added further that the leaders of the rebellion openly affronted the *Kunwars* or his heirs.[62] It may be recalled that earlier, a large number of people had petitioned, that if they were to be taxed it should be through their *Raja*. Later the *Raja's* agent placed a petition with the authorities to allow the *Raja* to farm the revenues of Jaintia, but this was rejected. At this stage it may appear that the *Raja* somewhere down the line might have influenced the people to rebel. Adding more to this it was seen that, with the refusal of the petition disturbances started. In light of the above developments it was expected therefore for the authorities to suspect that the *Raja* might have had a hand in exciting the outburst.[63] At one stage it was even argued that perhaps the *Raja* was under the influence of some fugitives of the Chittagong mutineers.[64] Steps were also taken to study whether the outbreak in Nowgong, where Lieutenant Singer lost his life had any direct effect in stimulating the insurrection.[65] The study revealed that there is no concrete evidence to show that such an alliance or a concert had taken place. Haughton, therefore, concluded that "no desire for a Raja caused the rebellion. The desire such as it was rather rose out of the circumstances which produced rebellion".[66]

Whatever might have been the case, the question of the ex-*Raja* being loyal was doubted and accordingly, steps were taken by the authorities to remove him from the frontier and to be detained at some place from where no further communication could be kept up between the *Raja* and the people of Jaintia. It was for this reason, that the *Raja* and his relatives were ordered to be removed to Dacca. The local officer, it was asserted, did not carry out those orders due to oversight and the ex-*Raja* was permitted to live in Sylhet where he had been residing since his withdrawal from Jaintiapur at the commencement of the outbreak.[67] At one stage during the course of the resistance, the *Kunwars* were brought to the hills with the motive of talking to those who were at arms and to convince them to give up the resistance. They had to be removed immediately as it was found out that their presence in the hills had excited the people all the more. Morton the Deputy Commissioner had even proposed to remove them from Sylhet to Calcutta.[68]

Long Term Effects

The British military operations and other methods of successfully suppressed the resistance. During the disturbance and afterwards, the police of the Khasi Hills envinced great activity and vigilance in bringing about the establishment of authority and order throughout the district.[69] The people recovered fast from their temporary poverty during the disturbances. *Hats* were better attended than before and agriculture, trade and commerce recovered.[70] With the pacification of the hills, the Commissioner of Assam was directed by the Government of Bengal to submit a draft set of rules framed on the basis of the existing laws for the local administration of the Jaintia Hills. Haughton pointed out that the operation of the general laws of India should be restricted and only those laws should be enforced that might be applicable to the territory. The authorities taking this point into consideration, not only retained the office of the *Dalois*, but also empowered them to try civil and criminal cases except those involving Europeans or people who are not Jaintias. The suits were to be tried in open *durbars* in the presence of a plaintiff and a defendant or their representatives and with not less than three respectable witnesses. The Deputy Commissioner's court would not entertain any appeal and the former could call for the proceedings of the local courts.[71] Cases involving fines to a limit of rupees fifty were entrusted to the Dalois.[72] The Assistant Commissioner of the subdivision was invested with full powers of a Magistrate in criminal justice.

One significant development in the post 1860–1863 period was the building of a new civil and military headquarter at Shillong.[73] Earlier there were other proposals to shift the headquarter to other places other than Cherrapunji because of the practical disadvantages that it received an extraordinary amount of rainfall.[74] T. Fisher, Superintendent of Cachar had wanted the Cantonment to be set up near Nongkrem,[75] while Scott preferred Mylliem.[76] W.J. Allen proposed Laitlyngkot to the Government.[77] The suggestion to shift the civil and military station from Cherrapunji to Shillong was first mooted by Rowlatt in September 1860.[78] In choosing Shillong, Rowlatt was having in mind of its central location and would be more easily accessible to the people than the existing station.[79] The disturbances in Jaintia Hills and the need to distribute and expedite troops quickly and effectively throughout British territories in case of emergencies had made the subject of locating European troops in the hills to be reviewed immediately.[80] A committee of enquiry was appointed to look into the matter, comprising Colonel Richardson commanding the troops at Cherrapunji and Morton the Deputy Commissioner, to report on the suitability of the proposed site.[81] The northern slopes of the Shillong range and the plateau of Yewduh were recommended. Taking all these into considerations the Lieutenant Governor of Bengal, Sir John Peter Grant sanctioned on 29 October, 1861, the transfer of the Deputy Commissioner's establishment from Cherrapunji to Shillong.[82]

In the height of the second Jaintia rising in 1862, Showers submitted his report to the Government of Bengal where Yewduh was proposed to be the civil station of the district. He pointed out that the adjoining locality of Shillong and Yewduh were in favourable position for maintaining control over both Khasi and Jaintia Hills.[83] He argued that the Jaintias were still a military problem and concluded that the Jaintia disturbances would render it necessary to keep a strong military force in the new proposed site.[84] On the 1 July, 1864, H.S. Bivar, the Deputy Commissioner of the Khasi and Jaintia Hills on the instruction of the Government transferred formally the headquarter of the district to Shillong.[85] But it was only in April 1866 that the civil departments from Cherrapunji were transferred to Shillong and the police, the jails, the treasury office and the Deputy Commissioner's office were finally established.[86]

Meanwhile in view of the necessity for more visible administration draft revenue rules were made. The *Daloi* was to collect a tax of one rupee per house and twenty per cent of the amount collected would go to him as a remuneration for his effort. The income tax was to be collected only where it was leviable.[87] It was only in January 1886 that the house tax on the Jaintias was raised to rupees two.[88] The authorities took step to communicate and explain the rise in tax to the people, so that it would not lead to any kind of reaction as it had earlier in 1860. By this later period it was reported that the Jaintias had started to evade the payment of these taxes; but in a different manner altogether. The house tax was levied on each house and not on households. The Jaintias understanding the technical aspect of the form of payment, started to construct houses with connecting roofs in order to pay just one tax. By 1889–90 the Government found out that the number of tax paying houses had decreased by 648 to that which were enumerated in 1884–85.[89] The Deputy Commissioner Major H. Maxwell believed that around a thousand householders evaded the payments in this fashion. In this regard, Maxwell asked the Chief Commissioner's sanction to issue an order that semi-detached houses should be taxed as two houses.[90]

The other administrative arrangements were in the police department. It was held that the police duties were to be undertaken by a body of regular police of hundred thrity-one in strength; that would include two inspectors, three sub-inspectors, thirteen head constables and hundred thirteen constables, which were again to be assisted by the village authorities including the *Dalois, Sardars, Pators* and the *Langdohs*.[91] The strength of the police would be sufficient for the requirements of the country. By the application of the provision of Act XXII of 1869 to the Khasi and Jaintia Hills, General Regulations and Acts including special rules for Administration of Justice was introduced.[92] Apparently these draft rules were only brought into force in the district from 12 August, 1872 following a general exclusion of the hill tribes of India from the general rules and regulations in force in British India.[93] H.S. Bivar the Deputy Commissioner of Khasi and Jaintia Hills in his correspondence to the Personal Assistant to the Governor General's Agent, North-East Frontier pointed out that the rules which were brought into force from 1872 onwards were successful and no difficulty had arisen in connection with them.[94] The native police consisting of *Sardars, Dalois, Pators* and *Langdohs* were reported to have conducted their duties in a satisfactory manner. The *Durbars* had also conducted their administration of criminal justice properly. Regarding the civil rules, steps were taken by the authorities to impress upon the officers about their responsibility in discharging their duties justly and impartially.[95]

From the above discussion it may be assumed that the pacification of the hills was complete and the rules that were framed for the Jaintia Hills in particular were easily understood by the people. The Government also expected that the administrative measures that were enforced would give further satisfaction. It was therefore, on these general principles of administration that Jaintia Hills was reformed. The policy of direct management, by resident European officers proved successful.[96] It was as a result of these new measures which governed the hills that the people eventually settled down to accept British rule. Where grievances would arise these would be referred to the authorities or to the courts of law and never again took the form of an armed resistance. The history of the Jaintias from this date onwards till 1947 was another case of passive submission to the might of British imperialism.

REFERENCES

1. Bengal Judicial Proceedings, No. 351, 13 February, 1863; Trial by the Special Commissioner under Act XI of 1857 held in the Cossayah and Jynteah Hills during January 1863.
2. Annual Report on the Administration of Bengal Presidency for 1863–1864, p. 109.
3. Bengal Judicial Proceedings, 9 July, 1862, Morton to Major Agnew, Judicial Commissioner incharge of the Commissioner's Office in Assam, Gowhatty, p. 67.
4. Bengal Judicial Proceedings, No. 98, October, 1862; Morton to Agnew, p. 67; also in *Selections of Records of the Government of Bengal*, Morton to Agnew, 9 July, 1862, p. 214.
5. Ibid.
6. Bengal Judicial Proceedings, 9 July, 1862, Morton to Agnew, p. 67.
7. Ibid.
8. Ibid.
9. Ibid.
10. *Selections of Records of the Government of Bengal*, No. 30(c), 3 July, 1863, J.C. Haughton to the Secretary to the Government of Bengal.
11. Bengal Judicial Proceedings, 9 July, 1862, Morton to Agnew.
12. Ibid.
13. Ibid.
14. Ibid.
15. Ibid.
16. *Selections of Records of the Government of Bengal*, 28 February, 1862, No. 20; Henry Hopkinson, Agent Governor General, North-East Frontier to the Secretary to the Government of Bengal.
17. Ibid.
18. *Selections of Records of the Government of Bengal*, 8 June 1862; G.D. Showers, Commissioner of the Cossayah and Jynteah Hills to the Secretary to the Government of Bengal.
19. Ibid.
20. Ibid.
21. Home Public Correspondence, No. 59, 25 September 1862; also in D.R. Syiemlieh's *British Administration in Meghalaya, Policy and Patterns*, p. 94.

22. Ibid.
23. *Selections of Records of the Government of Bengal,* No. 111; 9 April 1862; E.A. Rowlatt to the Secretary to the Government of Bengal.
24. *Selections of Records of the Government of Bengal,* 8 June, 1862; Showers to the Secretary to the Government of Bengal, p. 164.
25. Ibid.
26. Ibid.
27. Ibid.
28. Ibid.
29. Ibid.
30. Ibid.
31. Selection of Records of the Government of Bengal, No. 9(c), 7 February, 1863; J.C. Haughton to the Secretary to the Government of Bengal.
32. Ibid.
33. Ibid.
34. Ibid.
35. Ibid.
36. Ibid.
37. Ibid.
38. Ibid.
39. Ibid.
40. Ibid.
41. *Abstract of Letters from India,* Judicial No. 34, 1863; also in D.R. Syiemlieh's op. cit., p. 95.
42. *Selection of Records of the Government of Bengal,* No. 1868, 6 March, 1863; E.H. Lushington to J.C. Haughton.
43. Bengal Judicial Proceedings, No. 98, October, 1862.
44. Ibid.
45. *Selections of Records of the Government of Bengal,* No. 1868, 6 March, 1863; E.H. Lushington to Colonel J.C. Haughton; also in D.R. Syiemlieh's, op. cit., p. 94.
46. Ibid.
47. Ibid.
48. Ibid.
49. Ibid.
50. Ibid.
51. Ibid.
52. *The Calcutta Gazette,* 24 November, 1869; p. 2067.
53. *Annual Report on the Administration of Bengal Presidency, 1863–1864,* p. 109; also in L.W. Shakespear, *The Assam Rifles,* p. 50.
54. D.R. Syiemlieh's, op. cit., p. 95.
55. *Annual Report on the Administration of Bengal Presidency, 1863–1864,* p. 109.
56. Ibid.
57. Bengal Judicial Proceedings, No. 106 and 287; 19 January, 1863; Major W. Agnew to the Secretary to the Government of Bengal.
58. Bengal Judicial Proceedings, No. 436 and 858, 30 January, 1863; J. Geoghegan, Secretary to the Government of Bengal to the Officiating Officer of Assam.

59. Ibid.
60. *Selections of Records of the Government of Bengal*, No. 7(c), 4 February, 1863; Haughton to the Secretary to the Government of Bengal.
61. *Selections of Records of the Government of Bengal*, No. 30(c), 3 July, 1863; Haughton to the Secretary to the Government of Bengal.
62. Ibid.
63. Ibid.
64. The 34th Native Infantry stationed at Chittagong mutinied and started to march towards Cachar through Tripura and Sylhet. Fierce battles were fought at Latu in the Karimganj district. In this fight Major Byang lost his life. The mutineers were dispersed later by Subehdar Ayodhya Singh. For more details, references made be made to *North-East India History Association's Proceedings*, the 2nd, 4th and 10th Sessions.
65. *Annual Report on the Administration of the Bengal Presidency 1861–1862*, p. 65.
66. *Selections of Records of the Government of Bengal*, No. 30(c), 3 July, 1863; Haughton to the Secretary to the Government of Bengal.
67. *Annual Report on the Administration of the Bengal Presidency, 1860–1861*, p. 137.
68. *Selections of Records of the Government of Bengal*, 28 October, 1862, Morton to the Officiating Secretary to the Government of Bengal.
69. *Annual Report on the Administration of the Bengal Presidency, 1863–1864*, p. 109.
70. Charles Wood collection, Mss Eur F 78/89/ Bundle 3, Clarke to Hopkinson, 28 February 1865; cited in D.R. Syiemlieh, op. cit., p. 95.
71. Bengal Judicial Proceedings, No. 129, June, 1865.
72. Bengal Judicial Proceedings, No. 131, June, 1865.
73. P.N. Dutta, *Impact of the West on the Khasis and the Jaintias*, p. 117.
74. D.R. Syiemlieh's, op. cit., p. 97.
75. Bentinck Papers, PWJF 2791/111; Fisher to Scott, 16 October 1830; cited in D.R. Syiemlieh, op. cit., p. 97.
76. Ibid. Scott to Swinton, 20 October, 1830.
77. W.J. Allen, *Report on the Cossyah and Jynteah Hill Territory*, pp. 75–77.
78. D.R. Syiemlieh's, op. cit., p. 97.
79. Ibid.
80. P.N. Dutta, op. cit., p. 117.
81. D.R. Syiemlieh's, op. cit., p. 98.
82. Ibid.
83. P.N. Dutta, op. cit., p. 119.
84. D.R. Syiemlieh's, op. cit., p. 98; also in P.N. Dutta, op. cit., p. 121.
85. Assam Secretariat Records, No. 180, 28 April, 1866; H. Hopkinson to the Secretary to the Government of Bengal.
86. Bengal Judicial Proceedings, No. 133, June, 1865.
87. D.R. Syiemlieh's, op. cit., p. 149.
88. Assam Secretariat Records, R.A.P. (Revenue and Agriculture Proceedings) No. 23, April 1890; cited in D.R. Syiemlieh's, op. cit., p. 150.
89. Ibid.
90. Foreign Department (A) No. 312, November, 1874; Administrative Report by the D.C. for the Khasi and Jaintia Hills ending 31 March, 1874; also in H.K. Barpujari (ed.) *The Comprehensive History of Assam*, Vol. IV, p. 163.

91. Ibid.
92. Bengal Judicial Proceedings, No. 4, October, 1873; also in D.R. Syiemlieh, op. cit., p. 96.
93. Bengal Judicial Proceedings, No. 4, October, 1873.
94. Ibid.
95. Ibid.
96. Alexander Mackenzie, *History of the Relations of the Government with the Hill Tribes of the North-East Frontier of Bengal*, p. 243.

Chart-A (1862)

Trials by the Special Commissioner Under Act XI of 1857, held in the Cossyah and Jynteah Hills During December 1862

By whom tried	Date	Name of Prisoner	Name of Father	Resident of	Charge	Findings	Sentences
Colonel H.F. Downsford C.B.	24.12.1862	Oomun	Ooja	Nongjngee	Rebellion Captured In arms	Guilty	Three years imprisonment with labour in Irons.
"	24.12.1862	Ookat	Ooksan	Takinyung	"	"	have been promised pardon by Havildar
"	24.12.1862	Oobur	Ooman	"	"	"	Chunder Beer 44th Regiment
"	24.12.1862	Ookar	Oomie	"	"	"	Native Infantry on conditions of showing where grains was concealed.
"	24.12.1862	Ookiang	Ooffet	Jowai	Rebellion and instigating rebellion against the Queen.	"	To be hanged by the neck until he was dead, 30 Dec. 1862

Source: Bengal Judicial Proceedings, No. 214, 4 March 1863; J.C. Haughton to the Secretary to the Government of Bengal.

Chart-B (1863)

Trial by the Special Commissioner Under Act XI of 1857, held in the Cossyah and Jynteah Hills During January 1863

By whom tried	Date	Name of Prisoner	Name of Father	Resident of	Charge	Findings	Sentences
Col. H.F. Dunsford	24.1.1863	Suckun Murrea	Ookat	Mobekun	Rebellion & instigating Rebellion	Guilty	Two years imprisonment with labour in irons.
"	24.1.1863	Soowar	Ooriang	Rumbai	"	"	"
Capt. B.W.D. Morton	16.1.1863	Oossa Maratteang	Ooriang	"	Rebellion against the British	"	Hung by the neck till he be dead.
"	19.1.1863	Juggut	Soomet	Munsow	"	"	Five years imprisonment with hard labour in irons.
"	"	Oossa	Soomet	"	"	"	1 year
"	"	Summet	Biong	"	"	"	3 years
"	"	Shilliong	Nunka	"	Assisting and comforting those in rebellion	"	6 months
"	"	Ooyang	Ookiang	Soosen Poonjee	Rebellion against the British	"	5 years
"	"	Ooriang	Jatta	Jowai	"	"	"

contd on next page...

contd from previous page...

By whom tried	Date	Name of Prisoner	Name of Father	Resident of	Charge	Findings	Sentences
Cap. B.W.D. Morton	19.1.1863	Oorong	Boiraghy	Nurteng	Rebellion against the British	Guilty	5 years
"	"	Sazzar	Oopet	"	"	"	"
"	20.1.1863	Ooram	Oomon	Jowai	"	"	7 years
"	"	Oobor	Oomon	"	"	"	5 years
"	"	Ooriang	Oorong	"	"	"	"
"	"	Ookiang	Oomon	"	"	"	"
"	"	Oorietta	Oosing	"	"	"	"
"	"	Ooosan	Ooriang	"	"	"	"
"	"	Oosing	Oosai	"	"	"	"

Source: Bengal Judicial Proceedings, No. 351, January 1863; Trial by the Special Commissioner Under Act XI of 1857 held in Cossyah and Jynteah.

Chart-C (1863)

Trial by the Special Commissioner Under Act XI of 1857, held in the Cossyah and Jynteah Hills During February 1863

By whom tried	Date	Name of Prisoner	Name of Father	Resident of	Charge	Findings	Sentences
1. Lt. Colonel J.C. Haughton	1.2.1863	Manick	Ooreang	Lamin	Rebellion		No. 6 and No. 8, boys are released. No. 5 is subject to Epileptic fits having been twice attacked under trials and who has urged that he is unable to take care of himself and have taken no prominent parts, but simply defended themselves when surprised by the police, considering also that the rest of their village has submitted, I pardon them.
2. "	"	Oochoe	Oosnai	"	"		
3. "	"	Labhan	Oosatee	"	"	That the prisoners are rebels though probably not of the worse stamp	
4. "	"	Manick	Ooman	"	"		
5. "	"	Ookatt	Oolong	"	"		
6. "	"	Oochoe	Ooreang	"	"		
7. "	"	Ookong	Jetta	"	"		
8. "	"	Ooram	Oosnai	"	"		
9. "	"	Oohet	Ooreang	"	"		

Source: Bengal Judicial Proceedings, No. 127; 28 March, 1863; Trials by the Special Commissioner Under Act XI of 1857 held in Cossyah and Jynteah Hills.

Chart-D (1863)

Cases Under Act XI of 1857, decided during the month of February 1863

	Date	Name of Officer trying	Name of Prisoner	Name of Father	Resident of	Charge	Findings	Sentences
1.	1.2.1863	Capt. B.W.D. Morton	Oochai	x	Mokla Nongba	Rebellion against British Govt.	Rebellion against British Govt.	Five years imprisonment with hard labour in Irons
	"	"	Omi	x	"	"	"	x
2.	"	"	Ookut	x	"	"	"	For three years with hard labour in irons.
	"	"	Oossyang	x	"	"	"	Six months imprisonment with hard labour in irons.
3.	19.2.1863	"	Ookat	Oyoung	"	"	"	One year imprisonment with hard labour in Irons.

Note: (Memorandum from Capt. B.W.D. Morton dt. 23 April 1863). "Mr. Shadwell states that these men have not up to date been received at the Cherra Jail. I know that they were prisoners made over to the Havildar".

Source: Bengal Judicial Proceedings, No. 303, February 1863; Statement of cases under Act XI of 1857 decided by Captian B.W.D. Morton, Special Commissioner under the Act.

6

Conclusion

The Jaintia Resistance was entirely a tribal movement and cannot be equated with the other agrarian or peasant revolts that had taken place in other parts of India. The Jaintias did not revolt on agrarian issues nor did they fall under those exploited groups as the term 'peasant' would be understood in other societies. Their lands did not fall under the control of any landlord or *zamindars*, nor was the fight directed against any feudal lord. It was a clear case of resistance that was carried out by the people against British rule. It has been noted that though the war was spearheaded in some places by the traditional chiefs such as the *Dalois*, the *Pators* and other officials, they were joined in the fight by others who belonged to other professions such as the artisans, traders, merchants, farmers and others. That it was a tribal resistance there is no doubt because the people resisted the different enactments and legislations that were carried out by the British authorities. It may be pointed out that the general desire was to oust the British from Jaintia Hills and to revive back the legacy of the Jaintia *Raj*.

The solidarity that was shown during the war period was a clear indication that the Jaintias wanted to overthrow the foreign rule, though, this was to remain only as a hope. The Jaintias were badly equipped both in terms of arms, ammunition and food supplies. Those who took part in the struggle had no proper means of communicating with their fellow men. On the other hand, the British officials and military generals made use of the telegraph services and *dak* to send messages about the movement of the Jaintias. In this manner troops, guns and important provisions were moved in advance. Steps were taken to close *hats* in the territory of the Nongkrem and Khyriem Raja respectively.[1] A body of police was also placed at Puriang to prevent the Jaintias from getting supplies from the Khyriem territory.[2]

It may be recalled that during the course of the war, there was much talk and apprehension in the British camp that the Jaintias were seeking help from Burma and Russia[3] but apparently nothing seemed to have brought foreign help. The Jaintias carried out their struggle without any aid from outside.

Apart from the above problems the major weakness of the uprising came from the lack of proper understanding about the entire concept of resisting the British rule. There is no denying the fact that the Jaintias world view at that period was very limited. They did not have a clear knowledge about the strength of the British forces nor were they aware about the very basis on which British Imperialism was based. Further more the Jaintias did not have an alternative. They fought within the framework of the old social order. Jaintia converts to Christianity and the literates kept themselves away from the resistance movement and at times even remained loyal to the British authorities. This would explain why their settlements were attacked and burnt with the outbreak of the resistance. Since the number of converts was comparatively small, they were removed to Cherrapunji. There were instances where the *Dalois* assisted the British in procuring *coolies* in order to carry important supplies to the government troops.

From the number of battles that were fought, the siege of Surtiang at Nongkhlieh near Sutnga was considered to be one of the most intense. The oral tradition narrates that it was a decisive battle which changed the course of the resistance.[4] Strange enough, in the British military records, there was hardly anything mentioned about this battle. The Jaintias defending the fort was composed of armed men, coming from places such as Shangpung, Rymbai, Sutnga, from Nongkhlieh itself and some from neighbouring *Daloiships*. The British troops operated from a valley of the opposite side of the Surtiang fort. The fort was attacked, the Jaintias fought back gallantly, and this continued for six months. Seeing the seriousness of the resistance a large number of British soldiers were pressed into action. In the initial stages of the seige the British soldiers suffered reverse and the Jaintias made use of the deep ravines, which surrounded the fort to their advantage. A cloth merchant from Rymbai[5] after being paid a large amount of money gave information to the British troops about the secret path leading to the fort. The soldiers reached the stockade and it was just a matter of time that the strategies of the Jaintias were known. Manik Daloi of Sutnga who was operating the cane brake[6] from where arrows were fired, died fighting against the British.

Events took a different turn when U Kiang Nangbah fell ill and retired to Umkara. He was captured through wilful betrayal and was surrendered to the Military Tribunal, who found him guilty and passed the death sentence, the details of which have already been discussed. After he was declared dead by hanging, his body was handed over to Ka Hat Lyngdoh[7] and tradition has it that he was buried near a hillock called U Lum Ryngkaw, a place which is towards the south of the Tpep Pale locality in Jowai. The grave was dug by the army *sepoys*. The news of his capture and execution spread fast. His relatives who were all the time moving in the jungles and hiding, on knowing about the fate of U Kiang Nangbah came overground to carry out the rites meant for the departed soul. Later the body of U Kiang Nangbah was dug out and was cremated according to the traditional practices in the very place where he was buried. His bones were later taken and placed in another hillock called U Lum Mooliksoo.[8] This was in accordance with the Jaintia practice of placing human remains in a bone repository.

The death of U Kiang did not mean that the resistance was finally suppressed. In fact, places in the south such as Padu, Nongbarai, Umkiang and others saw serious fights and a large concentration of troops. It may be pointed out here that though the people were still carrying out the resistance, they were no longer organised. By the early part of 1863 most of the other leaders were either killed in encounter or surrendered and taken as prisoners. Some of these prominent leaders were: U Swar Sutnga, who died fighting till the last;

U Long Padu who died of sickness; U Mon Rymbai who was killed by the people near Nongbah and U Chey Rangbah, the trusted lieutenant of U Kiang who died in action. There were also others who surrendered after praying that their lives would be spared. They were U Bang Ralliang, U Bukher Pator Ralliang, U Woh Riang, U Mulon Mynso, U Kiang Sule and U Kat changpung.[9] The surrender and capture of the leaders was followed by a series of trials during the early part of 1863.[10] Except for one 'Ossa Maratteang' who was hanged[11] the others were either transported for life or sentenced for few years of imprisonment with labour in irons.[12]

The underlining meaning of the entire episode of the resistance movement was the political awakening of the people in their fight against British imperialism. According to J.B. Bhattacharjee, the movement was "a tremendous upheaval that had literally rocked the Jaintia Hills and shaken the citadel of colonial power in the north eastern hills."[13] Kiang Nangbah with his strong leadership qualities aroused the national sense by talking to the people in plain terms about their historic past. This had a binding force on the people in the formative stages of their resistance movement.

By 1864 everything was quiet in the hills. The Jaintias had by then been defeated. The suppression of the movement led to the other developments for which the resistance was fought. Taxes were levied and the house tax was to become the chief source of revenue. The income tax was withdrawn but there were some other sources from which the British Government was able to collect revenue such as, excise, forest produce, elephant catching, fisheries and stamp duty. The comparative calm in the previously disturbed area encouraged the government of Bengal to renew its attempt to increase their revenue from the hills. It was for this reason that in 1865 and 1866 the Commissioner of Assam was asked to enquire into the possibilities of assessing the cultivated lands. The Commissioner opposed the proposal and argued that the tax on the Jaintias would not only be unproductive but it would also disturb the mind of the Jaintias and would therefore doubt the intentions of the Government. It was also argued that the events of 1860 and 1862 were too immediate to be forgotten and the imposition of additional tax would upset the entire attempts of 'confidence building measures'.[14] Apprehension of future disturbances, compelled the government to abandon the proposal of a land tax and to stick to the indirect taxation as referred earlier.

The pacification of the hills led to a series of developments in the aftermath of resistance. Apart from the administrative measures, that have been discussed, there were other changes affecting where the society. The British rule brought about changes in the economy of the Jaintias. New crops, vegetables and fruits were introduced. These were cultivated extensively both for local consumption and for export. Potatoes, for instance, because of the enormous demand in Calcutta had led to its extensive cultivation in the Jaintia Hills. It may be mentioned that the Tuber was first introduced by the English in 1830 in the Khasi Hills. Trade and commerce started to pick up once again and Jaintiapur continued to be an important mercantile centre. With time the local economy was integrated into the colonial economy through the weekly markets which were held on successive days of the eight day week.[15] Despite a closer administrative link with Assam, the greater portion of the trade was carried on with Sylhet. This was mainly because the trade with Assam was comparatively insignificant being principally a barter trade.[16] On the whole the trade with Sylhet was about equally balanced. Though the region has vast deposits of coal in areas such as Amwi, Lakadong, Narpuh, Sutnga and Chermang which was estimated to yield about 1,100,000 tons,[17] it had not been explored. Perhaps the expense of carriage had prevented it from being of much commercial importance. No revenue was derived from these coal beds mentioned above. During the year 1877–1878, 5000 maunds of coal were quarried by the Executive Engineer of Sylhet for Government purposes. A small quantity was taken from Amwi by the European residents of Jowai for private consumption.[18] Iron ore from Jaintia Hills was also of an excellent quality. It was preferred to English iron by the Bengali blacksmith as a result of its malleability and being more easily worked. The peace that followed also led to the growth of a fair trade in iron articles such as *daos*, hoes, spears, arrowheads etc. manufactured by the Jaintia blacksmith.[19]

The other significant development was in the field of language and other practices. After the suppression of the uprising, the missionaries resumed their works. In the schools the Jaintias were taught in the Khasi vernacular but in the Roman alphabet, though Bengali and English were also retained in the curriculum. Since most of the educated Jaintia were either pro-British or converts to Christianity, they never questioned the authorities and the Church against such forms of imposition, nor did they take steps to develop their own language. Here it would not be wrong if stated that there was no initiative taken by the church to develop the indigenous vernacular language.[20] The missionaries also played an important role in strengthening the policies of the British Raj. In order to make the people submissive, the missionaries took certain measures to prevent the converts from attending and participating in their traditional festivals and rituals. The traditional practices were considered to go against the basic teachings of Christianity and therefore unlogical and in their view must be disbanded. This was a deliberate attempt on the part of the missionaries and with time it was noticed that the arms and weapons that were used in the traditional dance and other purposes, did not find their way into those houses which showed their loyalty and allegiance to the Church or the Government.[21] The backbone of the resistance was now crushed for ever, once the rift amongst the Jaintias had taken roots. It would moreover be an effective measure that no resistance would recur.

Another important change that followed the resistance was the construction of roads. This gained importance all the more when the proposal was approved to make Shillong into new civil and military headquarters.[22] The urgency to construct roads was realised when the headquarters of the district was shifted from Cherra to Shillong. In this context roads in Jaintia Hills and those between Jowai and other important areas like Mukhtapur, Jaintiapur, Sylhet, Nartiang and extending to the district of Nowgong in the Brahmaputra valley were worked out.[23] It was estimated that these constructions had resulted in the developments of the best system of roads among the hill districts of the North-East Frontier.[24] The importance of Jowai was seen all the more when Jowai was made into a sub-division in 1869 with an Assistant Deputy Commissioner stationed there.[25] The important towns of the district, Shillong, Jowai, and Cherra were also connected by telegraph communication system. Later the hills were integrated with the plain districts of Assam and the Surma valley when the headquarters of the Province was transferred to Shillong on 20 March 1874. One significant development in such forms of integration was that the system of administration remained undisturbed. The Khasi and Jaintia Hills were declared as 'Scheduled District' and were administered under the simple system of government and different than the plains districts.[26]

Thus going by the above discussion it appears that the Jaintia resistance of 1860–1863 had brought about momentous political, economic and social changes in Jaintia Hills. U Kiang Nangbah's role in the entire phase of the second outbreak is still remembered and cherished by all Jaintias as a struggle of patriotism and for national liberation. Kiang Nangbah has figured not merely as a freedom fighter but also as a prophet. Before he was hanged he proclaimed to the people that if his face turned east on the noose when he died, then the country would be free within one hundred years from British rule.[27] True to his words the country was free from the foreign yoke in 1947. U Kiang encouraged nationalism among the Jaintias. U Kiang Nangbah still lives in the hearts and minds of the Jaintias and inspires the people to accomplish the task which he could not do in nation building. A monument in memory of this Jaintia leader was built in 1969 by the Kiang Nangbah Memorial Fund. It stands today in the same place, 'Madiah Kmai Blai', where Kiang Nangbah was chosen by the *Dalois* and the Jaintia *ryots* to lead the people in their fight against British imperialism. At present there is an emerging appreciation on the role of U Kiang Nagbah and is being highlighted in many popular writings. The State Government of Meghalaya has declared 30 December as a State holiday, in order to show reverence on the death anniversary of the Jaintia leader. Every year a number of functions and ceremonies are organized both in Jowai and in the State capital Shillong, to mark the occasion and to pay tributes to the leader of the Jaintia resistance.

REFERENCES

1. Home Public Proceedings, No. 51(B), 24 July 1862; Morton to the Secretary, Government of Bengal; *The Friend of India*, 15 May 1862, 3 July, 1862.
2. Assam Secretariat Records, Commissioner's papers, File No. 408 of 1862; also in Home Public Proceedings, No. 56–57(b) 19 June, 1862, Morton to the Secretary, Government of Bengal.
3. *Selections of Records of the Government of Bengal* No. 17(c), 12 Nov. 1862; J.C. Haughton to the Officiating Secretary to the Government of Bengal.
4. Interview with Nichal Sutnga on 13.6.94 at Sutnga; discussion with late Prof. B. Pakem, Vice Chancellor of North-Eastern Hill University on 15.3.99 at Shillong.
5. H. Bareh, *History and Culture of the Khasi People*, p. 172.
6. Home Public Proceedings, Nos. 100–101(B), 12 April, 1862; Dunsford to Assistant Adjutant General.
7. Q. Sumer, *U Kiang Nangbah*, p. 23.
8. Ibid.
9. Ibid.
10. Bengal Judicial Proceedings, No. 351, Trials by the Special Commissioner under Act XI of 1857 held in the Cossyah and Jynteah Hills.
11. Ibid.
12. Ibid.
13. J.B. Bhattacharjee, op. cit., p. 184.
14. *Selections of Records of the Govt. of Bengal*, 8 June, 1862, Showers to Secretary to the Govt. of Bengal.
15. D.R. Syiemlieh, *British Administration in Meghalaya Policy and Pattern*, p. 101; L.S. Gassah, Trade Routes and trade Relations Between Jaintia Hills and Sylhet District in the Pre-Independence Period in *North-East India History Association*, 9th Session, 1988.
16. D.R. Syiemlieh, op. cit., p. 99.
17. W.F. Trotter, *Report on the Administration of Jowai for the Year Ending 31st March, 1878*, p. 18.
18. Ibid.
19. Ibid.
20. S.N. Lamare, The Cultural Transition of the Pnars, (Unpublished M.Phil. Dissertation), NEHU, 1994, p. 130.
21. Ibid.
22. P.N. Dutta, op. cit., p. 117.
23. W.W. Hunter, *A Statistical Account of Assam*, p. 232.
24. P.N. Dutta, op. cit., p. 117.
25. W.W. Hunter, op. cit., p. 243.
26. P.N. Dutta, op. cit., p. 117.
27. J.B. Bhattacharjee, 'The Jaintia Rebellion' in N.R. Ray (ed.) *Challenge*, p. 161; Hamlet Bareh, U Tirot Singh, p. 161; and also 'U Kiang Nangbah' in S.P. Sen's *Dictionary of National Biography*, Vol. 2, p. 23.

Appendix A

Home Public Proceedings, 19 May 1860, No. 39/40(A); From A.R. Young Esq. Secretary to the Government of Bengal to the Secretary to the Government of India, Home Department, dated Fort William, the 9th April 1860

Sir,

I am directed to inform here with the copy of two letters dated the 28th and 30th ... from the Commissioner of Assam reporting that the inhabitants of some of the villages in Jynteah have risen in arms to oppose to the collection of a house tax which have been ordered to be levied from them, and that a collision had occurred between some of these villagers and a party of troops sent out to coerce them in which several of the former were killed and wounded. A copy of the instruction is placed to the Commissioner is also herewith forwarded.

Earlier intimation of this rising has been received from the Commissioner of Dacca by Telegraph on Friday and the Military Department of the Government of India was addressed with a view to the speedy issue of orders to the officer commanding the East India Regiment to take that Regiment on towards Sylhet and to the officer commanding at Dacca to retain at that place until further orders, the Detachment of the 19th Regiment at Dacca.

The house tax to which the origin of this outbreak is attributed was imposed on the inhabitants of the Jynteah Hills by an order of the late Lt. Governor dated the 28th March 1859 No. 593 on a recommendation by Mr. Allen contained in para 263 to 269 of his report on the administration of the Cossaya and Jynteah Hill Territory. It was supposed that such a tax would be the one least distasteful and most easily collected. The preliminary cause was reported to have been completed in December last and the only difficulty in carrying out the measure which had been brought to notice and which consisted in the classification of the houses and their assessment at varying rates was removed by an order by the 26th January last which authorised the levying of the lowest rate of one rupee only on all houses. There was no apparent reason to apprehend any disturbances from the imposition of the tax and there seems some reasons to suspect that the villagers have been instigated to this rising by connections of the ex-Rajah of Jynteah.

I have the honour to be
Sir
Your most obedient Servant
A.R. Young
Secretary to the Government of Bengal

Appendix B

The Friend of India, 6 February, 1862

Upto 1858 the administration of the district was not conducted without expense, and in that year, after deputing a member of the Board of Revenue to the plan we imposed a house tax. They resisted, were punished and made to pay the tax. The impose which was no novelty had been made use of as a pretext, by the ex-Rajah to stir up intrigues for his restoration to a post he had voluntarily surrendered. An order ... forth that he should be removed to Dacca, but this was never obeyed by the local officers, "from oversight" as is naively confessed with official reports. It is thus that Bengal is governed and we ... nor wonder that the Jyntiah Khasias are once more in rebellion .... The cause of this uprising is said to be the new tax lately imposed upon them. But they said they would have been willing to bear this quietly had it not been for other burdens which are still more grevious. Of these others, they mentioned the lawlessness and corruption of the petty officials sent amongst them, who, they say fleece them without mercy; the disregard shown to their principal men and the fear they have for the security of their landed property which they imagined, government will take to itself, compelling them by decree to pay an annual rent.

The revolt would be a trifling matter if it did not complete the ring fence of hostile subjects as well as frontier tribes. The whole military strength in the vicinity was: at Sylhet 118 sepoys, at Jowai with Major Richardson who had command the province 100, at Cherrapunjee 100 guards scattered all over the district. There have now been sent up, 150 Kamroop and part of the E.I. Corps from Dacca; a wing of the 20 Punjabees from Barrackpore and 500 men of the Lucknow Regiment from Calcutta.

Appendix C

The Englishman, February 19, 1862

The little war in Assam is assuming larger proportions, and about to become expensive. The 33rd Regiment Native Infantry at Barrackpore commanded by Major Langmore is ordered to Assam, and will proceed there by river steamers in a few days. The 16th Native Infantry or Lucknow regiment, at Allipore, is ordered to hold itself in readiness to move at the shortest notice if required and finally General Showers leaves the Presidency for Assam, and to look up the whole frontier in that direction about 1st proximo. As all this expense and trouble has become necessary, in order to bring the savage tribes on the South-east border of Empire to quiet and submission, we hope that such treatment will be administered to them as will show them that government understand perfectly well the differences of treatment that ought to be exhibited in the case of a productive agrarian population in opposition to the laws and order and a horde of useless mountain savages who have no claim to mercy or political consideration except in as much as and when, they remain quiet and abstain from aggression. In other words the welfare and prosperity of the inhabitants of the plains and of our own territories are a test of our good government and a benefit to the community at large; whereas the annihilation of the tribes which are now causing so much trouble and expense so far from injuring a single interest in the country, would be a local, a provincial and a public gain. They should if possible, be treated in such a manner as to make them know this, and act accordingly. The embarrassed finances of the empire have to pay for the freaks of these savages; and we hope that General Showers will make an example of them.

Appendix D

Proceedings in the Case of Ookiang Nongba Charged with Rebellion

Present—Brigadier Dunsord, c.b. ... Commissioner Under
—Captain Morton ... Act XI of 1857

Reply of the Dependant—I shall speak the whole truth though I am hanged for it. I am neither Dolloye nor Pathor, I have attended to my fields. In the cold season I have traded with the Meekirs. Manick Dolloye held a durbar at Jowai, at which he informed all the ryots that by orders of Government the religious observances and the burning of the dead were prohibited. On hearing this I thought it was all up with us, and I therefore said at the durbar that I would not pay any tax.

Question by Brigadier Dunsford—How did Manick obtain his Dolloyeship?

The ryots of Lattober, Shermong, Jallong, Jowai, Padoo, and Pompadong, with whom lay the power of election, elected him.

Question by Brigadier Dunsford—Did you incite the other ryots not to pay tax?

All our poojah-arms were at Jallong, and I told all that we should give them in to the jemadar and flee to the jungles, as our worship had been stopped, without arms.

With this view we brought our arms to the guard and told the jemadar that we had come to give up our arms; that we would not fight with Government; but that, as our worship and the burning of our dead had been interfered with, we would flee to the jungles.

The sepoys of the guard fired on us and we ran off to the jungles. In the jungle near Jallong we held a durbar at which Manick attended. Manick gave orders that we were to fight for fifteen years, as we had no longer freedom to worship. In the evening after another durbar had been held, we went to fight the guard, at Jowai, but no fight took place owing to our fears. By order of Manick, a stockade was made at Jallong, Manick after this ran away to the Jowai guard. After the fall of the stockade, we ran to the neighbouring jungle. I was at the Munsow fight, but not at that of Ralliang. Oo Bang Dolloye was the leader at Ralliang.

He is still to the fore. For the last year I have never used arms. I have merely fled.

Question by Brigadier Dunsford—How then did you come by a Government musket?

They made me a Dolloye in the jungles and brought me the arms.

Question by Brigadier Dunsford—Where are the other muskets?

Ookma Langdo, of Jallong, has one. Oodran Sallo, of Jallong, has one. These two men between them have five Government muskets.

Question by Brigadier Dunsford—Do you know who killed the Nurteng Dolloye?

A man of Munsow whose name I forget, a ryot of Mullon Dolloye.

Question by Brigadier Dunsford—How came the stockades to be built?

The rebels built them. I have never been to them.

Question by Brigadier Dunsford—What stockades are there?

Oomkoi, Padoo, and I hear, Joori Sookkut.

Question by Brigadier Dunsford—At whose suggestion did the rebels refuse the offer of pardon?

The rebels acted on their own fears that perhaps they would be hanged. No one advised them to stay out. No one told us we would be pardoned. We were only told to submit.

We were told to come in and resettle, pay our revenue, and that it would be well for us. We did not hear that our poojah would be restored. I was present at the durbar held at Shamphoong by Rabun Sing, the Kowars, and Hajun Manick; also at one held at Nurteng by Ram Sing, Rabun Sing, and the Kowars.

All our twelve Dolloyes said that if our taxes were excused, and our Rajah restored, they would make friends, otherwise they would stay in the jungle.

Question by Captain Morton—You were dissatisfied with regard to interference with your religion, had you any other cause for rebellion?

We were not dissatisfied with the HOUSE TAX, but with the Income Tax. We raised a little produce from the ground and were taxed excessively.

Question by Brigadier Dunsford—How much Income Tax had you to pay?

Four Rupees.

Question by Brigadier Dunsford—Was any one to your knowledge taxed more than four Rupees?

I don't know.

Question by Captain Morton—Did you ever hear of their or of the darogah's taking money from the villagers on the pretence of tax?

No.

Question by Captain Morton—With the exception of interference with religion and the burning of the dead and of the Income Tax, had you any other cause for dissatisfaction?

No.

Question by Brigadier Dunsford—Did you know Major Rowlatt?

By name only.

Question by Captain Morton—Did actual interference with religious rites ever occur, or were you merely told by Manick that it would occur?

Manick, stating that it was by order of the Sahib, forbade the burning of the dead in the former place. The former place bordered on the Poonjee of Jowai.

Question by Captain Morton—Did Surkee Darogah ever interfere with your poojah at Jowai or Jallong?

Yes, both at Jowai and Jallong he forbade our burning the dead and poojah.

Question by Captain Morton—Did you ever complain of the acts of Manick or Surkee to the Sahib?

Yes, one went; Oossdea went to Cherra.

Question by Captain Morton—Did he go of himself or was he sent?

Of himself.

Question by Captain Morton—Did you believe that Manick acted under the Sahib's order?

(After fencing with the question Prisoner replies), I thought it was the Sahib's order.

Question by Captain Morton—What did the Sahib say when asked about the burning?

He said, "go and burn, who prevents you?"

Question by Captain Morton—When you heard that the Sahib had so spoken to one of your own villagers why did you still rebel?

The Dolloye prevented us.

Question by Captain Morton—Who has the power in the District, the Sahib or Dolloye?

The Sahib.

Question by Captain Morton—Then why did you not complain?

I don't know laws and regulations; so I took to the jungles.

Question by Brigadier Dunsford—Have you been on bad terms with Manick?

No.

Question by Brigadier Dunsford—You have heard that the Pathor said about his being imprisoned by you, what say you to that?

The rebels may have done so, but not by my order.

Question by Brigadier Dunsford—Where did you get the powder found near your house?

The men of Paddoo gave it to me. I have been there twice. The last time, four months ago, I went by the Khyrim territory by the village of Nourrong. We went in a party of 200. We went from Nongfloot by the Districts of Nongjoongee, Lattober, Shamphoong, and Shermong to the Mungut river.

Question by Captain Morton—With the exception of Surkee, did any of the police ever tyrannise over you?

No.

Question by Captain Morton—Did the police ever take your arms with which you were worshipping at Jallong?

Yes, Surkee Darogah did.

Question by Brigadier Dunsford—Who are the leaders of the rebellion?

Munsow District		..	..	Mullon
Shamphoong	"	..	..	Ookkatt
Ralliang	"	..	..	Oobang
Sattoonga	"	..	..	OoSawar
Rumbai	"	..	..	Oomonsa
Padoo and Pomtadon	"	of Jowai	..	Oo Long Langdo
Sath Poonjee	"	..	..	Oo Reah
Jowai	"	..	..	Oolloia, brother of Ookiang Pathor

Memorandum from Major J.C. Haughton, Officiating Agent of the Governor-General, on Special Duty—(No. 3 C, dated the 13th January 1863)

Copy of examination of Ookiang Nongba referred to in Captain Morton's letter dated 6th January, forwarded to the Secretary to the Government of Bengal, for the information of the Hon'ble the Lieutenant-Governor.

Bibliography

I. Primary Sources

Unpublished Documents

(a) Archival

(i) National Archives of India, New Delhi

(a) Home Public Proceedings, 1860–1874.

(b) Home Public Consultations & Proceedings, 1860–1863.

(c) Home Political Proceedings, 1862–1863.

(ii) State Archives, Government of West Bengal, Calcutta

(a) Bengal Judicial Proceedings, 1860–1863.

(b) Bengal Political Consultations, 1832–1835.

(c) Bengal Political Proceedings, 1860–1862.

(d) Bengal General Proceedings, 1868.

(iii) Assam State Archives, Guwahati

(a) Letters received from the Government of Bengal, 1824.

(b) Bengal Government Papers, 1835.

(c) Dacca Commissioner's Papers, 1860.

(d) Assam Commissioner's Papers, 1860.

(e) Letters issued from the Government, 1861.

(f) Foreign Department Letters, 1864–1866.

(g) Judicial Commissioner's Paper, 1864, 1865, 1866.

(h) Letters issued to the Government, 1865–1866.

(i) Board of Revenue Papers, 1871.

(j) Lists of pre- 1874 files received from the Government of Bengal.

(k) Lists of pre-1874 files received from Dacca Commissioner's Office.

Published

(a) Documents, Reports and Memoirs

Abstract of Letters received from India 1861–1863.

Aitchison, C.U. *A Collection of Treatise, Engagements and Sanads*, Vol. I, Calcutta, 1862, Vol. II, Calcutta, 1872.

Allen, W.J. *Report on the Administration of the Cossyah and Jynteah Hill Territory*, Calcutta, 1858, Reprinted, Shillong, 1903.

Allen, B.C. *Gazetteer of the Khasi and Jaintia Hills, Garo Hills, Lushai Hills*, Shillong, 1905.

Annual Report on the Administration of the Bengal Presidency during the year 1859–1860; 1860–1861; 1861–1862; 1862–1863; 1863–1864.

Bradley-Birt, F.B. *Sylhet Thackery*, London, 1911.

Firminger, W.K. *Sylhet District Records*, Vol. I, Shillong, 1913.

Heath, A.E. *Tour Diary of the Sub-Divisional Officer, Jowai, for the month of November and December 1882.*

Mills, A.J.M. *Report on the Khasi and Jaintia Hills*, Calcutta, 1853, Reprinted Shillong, 1901, Reprinted.

Pemberton, R.B. *Report on the Eastern Frontier of British India*, Calcutta, 1835, Reprinted Gauhati, 1966.

Selections of Records, Government of Bengal, Papers Relating to the Disturbances in the Cossyah and Jynteah Hills, No. XXXIX, Part I and II, Calcutta, 1864.

The Imperial Gazetteer of India, Provincial Series, Eastern Bengal and Assam, New Delhi, Reprinted, 1989.

Thorton, J.H. *Memories of Seven Campaigns*, Archibald Constable and Co., Westminster, 1895.

Trotter, W.F. *Report on the Administration of Jowai for the Year Ending 31 March 1878*, Calcutta, 1878.

Wilson, H.H. *Documents Illustrative of the Burmese War*, Calcutta, 1827.

Young, W.G. *Report on the Police of the Chittagong Division for 1862*, Calcutta, 1862.

(b) Gazette and Newspapers

1. *The Calcutta Gazetteer*, 1835–1873.
2. *The Friend of India*, 1860–1864.
3. *The Dacca Chronicle*, 1860–1864.
4. *The Englishman*, 1860–1864.

II. Secondary Sources

Acharyya, N.N. *Historical Documents of Assam and Neighbouring States* (Original Records in English), New Delhi, 1983.
Ali, S.M. *The History of Jaintia*, Dacca, 1954.
Bareh, H. *The History and Culture of the Khasi People*, Calcutta, 1967.
Barkataki, S. (Ed.) *Tribes of Assam*, New Delhi, 1969.
Barkataki, M.S. *British Administration in North-East India (1826–1874): A Study of Their Social Polity*, Delhi, 1985.
Banerjee, T. *Various Bengal, Aspects of Modern History*, Calcutta, 1985.
Barpujari, H.K. *Problems of the Hill Tribes: North-East Frontier 1843–72*, Vol. I, Gauhati, 1970.
Barpujari, H.K. *et al. Political History of Assam, Vol. I, 1826–1919*, Gauhati, 1977.
Barpujari, H.K. (Ed.), *The Comprehensive History of Assam*, Vol. II & IV, Guwahati, 1992.
Bertrand, G. *Secret Lands Where Women Reign*, London, 1958.
Bhattacharjee, J.B. *Social and Polity Formation in Pre-Colonial North-East India*, New Delhi, 1991.
Bose, Manilal. *Historical and Constitutional Documents of North-East India 1824–1973*, Delhi, 1979.
Buckland, C.E. *Bengal Under the Lieutenant Governors*, Vol. I, Calcutta 1901, Reprinted, New Delhi, 1976.
Chakravorty, B.C. *British Relations With the Hill Tribes of Assam Since 1858*, Calcutta, 1964.
Chandra, B. *et al. India's Struggle For Independence 1857–1947*, Calcutta, 1964.
Chattopadhyaya, S.K. *The Jaintias: Socio-Political Institutions of Jaintia Hills*, New Delhi, 1988.
Chaudhuri, K.C. *History of Modern India*, Calcutta, 1983.
Choudhury, J.N. *The Khasi Canvas*, Shillong, 1978.

Das Gupta, P.K. *Life and Culture of Matrilineal Tribes of Meghalaya*, New Delhi, 1984.

Desai, A.R. (Ed.) *Peasant Struggle in India*, Bombay, 1979.

—. *Social Background of Indian Nationalism*, Mumbai, 1998.

Deb Roy, H.L. *A Tribe in Transition: Jaintias of Meghalaya*, New Delhi, 1981.

Dutta, P.N. *Impact of the West on the Khasis and Jaintias*, New Delhi, 1982.

Dutta, R.C. *The Economic History of India*, Delhi, Reprinted, 1990.

Gait, E. *History of Assam*, Calcutta, 1967.

Gurdon, P.R.T. *The Khasis*, New Delhi, 1987.

Guha, Ranaji. *Elementary Aspect of Peasants Insurgency in Colonial India*, Delhi, 1983.

Hunter, W.W., *A Statistical Account of Bengal*, Vol. XIV, London, 1877, Reprinted, Delhi, 1976.

—. *A Statistical Account of Assam*, Vol. II, London, 1879, Reprinted, Delhi, 1972.

Kling, Blair. *The Blue Mutiny: Indigo Disturbance in Bengal 1850–1862*, Calcutta, 1977.

Lahiri, R.M. *Annexation of Assam*, Calcutta, 1975.

Lewis, J.H.T. *The Bengal Police Guide, Containing the Circulars and Memos of the Inspector General of Police from 1862–1866*, Calcutta, 1867.

Mackenzie, A. *History of the Relations of the Government with the Hill Tribes of the North-East Frontier of Bengal*, Calcutta, 1884, Reprinted, New Delhi,

Mahajan, V.D. *India Since 1526*, New Delhi, 1984.

Metcalf, T. *The Aftermath of Revolt: India, 1857–1870*, Princeton, 1965.

Morris, J.H. *The History of the Welsh Calvinistic Methodists Foreign Mission to the End of the Year 1904*, New Delhi, 1996.

Ray, N.R. *et al. Challenge: A Saga for India's Struggle for Freedom*, New Delhi, 1984.

Sarkar, Jayanta; B. Dutta Ray (ed). *Social and Political Institutions of the Hill People of North-East India*, Calcutta, 1990.

Sen, S.P. *Dictionary of National Biography*, Vol. 2, 1973.

Sen, Soumen. *Religion in North-East India*, New Delhi, 1992.

—. *Social and State Formation in Khasi-Jaintia Hills*, Delhi, 1985.

Shadap-Sen, N.C. *The Origin and Early History of the Khasi-Synteng People*, Calcutta, 1981.

Shakespear, L.W. *The Assam Rifles*, Aizawl, Reprinted, 1977.

Singh, J.P.; Nisar Ahmed (ed). *Coinage and Economy of North-Eastern States of India*, Memoirs Series No. 7, The Numismatic Society of Varanasi, 1980.

Stokes, Eric. *The Peasant Armed: The Indian Revolt of 1857*, Oxford, 1986.

Sumer, Q.*U Kiang Nangbah bad Ka Jingialeh Ka Ri Jaintia Na Ka Bynta Ka Jinglaitluid*, Jowai

Syiemlieh, D.R. *British Administration in Meghalaya: Policy and Pattern*, New Delhi, 1989.

Journals and Articles

Banerjee, A.C. "Jaintia" in H.K. Barpujari (ed.) *The Comprehensive History of Assam*, Vol. II, Guwahati, 1992.

Bareh, H. "U Kiang Nangbah" in *Dictionary of National Biographies*, edited by S.P. Sen, Vol. II, Calcutta, 1973.

Bhattacharjee, J.B. "Brahmanical Myths, Royal Legitimation and the Jaintia State Formation" in *Journal of Social Sciences and Humanities*, North-Eastern Hill University, Vol. III, No. I.

—. "Mutiny in Cachar: A Survey of the Local Sources" in *Proceedings of the North-East India History Association*, 4th Session, 1983.

—. "Genesis and Patterns of British Administration in the Hill Areas of North-Eastern India" in *Proceedings of the Indian History Congress*, 36th Session, 1975.

—. "The Jaintia Rebellion" in N. R. Ray *et al. Challenge: A Saga for India's Struggle for Freedom*, New Delhi, 1984.

Barman, S. "Agrarian Relations in Goalpara during British Regime with Special Reference to Peasant Movement", in *Proceedings of North-East India History Association*, 10th Session, 1989.

Barpujari, H.K. "Facts behind the Jaintia Rebellion 1862–1864" in *Journal of Indian History*, Vol. 51, Part I, 1973.

Dutta, S. "An Anti-British Alliance of the North-East—That Failed" in *Proceedings of North-East India History Association*, 8th Session, 1987.

Gassah, L.S. "Trade Routes and Trade Relations Between Jaintia Hills and Sylhet District in the Pre-Independence Periods", in *Proceedings of North-East India History Association*, 9th Session, 1988.

Gatphoh, A. "Education in Jaintia Hills (1854–1897)" in *Proceedings of North-East India History Association*, 11th Session, 1990.

Goswami, S. "A Fresh Look at the Jaintia Rebellion" in *Social Scientist*, Vol. 3, No. 2, February, 1985.

—. "The Raij Mels: Their Historic Role in Peasant Movements of Assam" in *Proceedings of North-East India History Association*, 10th Session, 1989.

Hussain, Imdad. "A Mid-Nineteenth Century View of Assam: The Little Known Diary of Sergeant Major George Carter" in *Proceedings of North-East India History Association*, 10th Session, 1989.

Kalita, R.C. "Immigrant to Assam: British Policy and Assamese Middle Class 1826-1900" in *Proceedings of North-East India History Association*, 13th Session, 1993.

—. "The Phulaguri Uprising of 1861: A Peasant Mass Movement" in *Proceedings of North-East India History Association*, 10th Session, 1989.

Lamare, Shobhan. "British Military Operations in the Jaintia Uprising of 1860" in *Proceedings of North-East India History Association*, 17th Session, 1997.

Lindsay, Robert. *Anecdotes of an Indian Life*, edited with an Introduction by D.R. Syiemlieh, Shillong, 1998.

Pakem, B. "The Socio-Political System of the Jaintia Tribe of Assam: An Analysis of Continuity and Change", in K.S. Singh (ed), *Tribal Situation in India*, 1972.

Passah, P.M. "The First Two Anglo-Jaintia Wars", in *Proceedings of North-East India History Association*, 13th Session, 1993.

Ray, B.D. "An Aspect of North-East Frontier Policy of Raj: An Overview", in *Proceedings of North-East India History Association*, 6th Session, 1985.

Sangma, M.S. "Last Resistance of the Garos to British Imperialism, 1872", in *Proceedings of North-East India History Association*, 10th Session, 1989.

Singh, J.P. "Jayantia Coins and the Koch Historical Tradition: An Examination", *Numismatic International,* Vol. 22, No. 5, May 1988.

Syiemlieh, D.R. "Leaves from the Past: A Soldier's Account", in *Khasi Studies,* Vol. V, No. 2, July–September, 1991.

—. "Leaves from the Past: Thorton's Account of the Jaintia Resistance", in *Khasi Studies,* Vol. VI, No. 3, October–December, 1992.

Unpublished Manuscript

Lamare, Shobhan. "The Cultural Transition of the Pnars from the Middle of the 19th Century to the First Half of the 20th Century". (Unpublished M. Phil Dissertation, NEHU, 1994).

Interviews

	Name	Place	Date
1.	Listerford Lamare	Jowai	- 20.3.96
2.	Kistobin Rymbai	Jowai	- 28.2.94
3.	Omarlin Kyndiah	Shillong	- 15.7.99
4.	R. Nongtdu	Jowai	- 31.5.96
5.	S.M. Roy Shilla	Jowai	- 04.6.96
6.	Nichal Sutnga	Sutnga	- 13.6.96
7.	B.N. Lamare	Jowai	- 16.6.96
8.	Don Dkhar	Nartiang	- 12.8.96
9.	Ridon Dkhamein	Nartiang	- 13.6.96
10.	R.S. Tariang	Jowai	- 13.6.96
11.	B. Pakem	Shillong	- 20.3.99